The Thoughts of My Boxer

2020 Daily Planner

A DAY TO A PAGE

2020

January

S	M	T	W	T	F	S
			1	2	3	4
5	6	7	8	9	10	11
12	13	14	15	16	17	18
19	20	21	22	23	24	25
26	27	28	29	30	31	

February

S	M	T	W	T	F	S
						1
2	3	4	5	6	7	8
9	10	11	12	13	14	15
16	17	18	19	20	21	22
23	24	25	26	27	28	29

March

S	M	T	W	T	F	S
1	2	3	4	5	6	7
8	9	10	11	12	13	14
15	16	17	18	19	20	21
22	23	24	25	26	27	28
29	30	31				

April

S	M	T	W	T	F	S
			1	2	3	4
5	6	7	8	9	10	11
12	13	14	15	16	17	18
19	20	21	22	23	24	25
26	27	28	29	30		

May

S	M	T	W	T	F	S
					1	2
3	4	5	6	7	8	9
10	11	12	13	14	15	16
17	18	19	20	21	22	23
24	25	26	27	28	29	30
31						

June

S	M	T	W	T	F	S
	1	2	3	4	5	6
7	8	9	10	11	12	13
14	15	16	17	18	19	20
21	22	23	24	25	26	27
28	29	30				

July

S	M	T	W	T	F	S
			1	2	3	4
5	6	7	8	9	10	11
12	13	14	15	16	17	18
19	20	21	22	23	24	25
26	27	28	29	30	31	

August

S	M	T	W	T	F	S
						1
2	3	4	5	6	7	8
9	10	11	12	13	14	15
16	17	18	19	20	21	22
23	24	25	26	27	28	29
30	31					

September

S	M	T	W	T	F	S
		1	2	3	4	5
6	7	8	9	10	11	12
13	14	15	16	17	18	19
20	21	22	23	24	25	26
27	28	29	30			

October

S	M	T	W	T	F	S
				1	2	3
4	5	6	7	8	9	10
11	12	13	14	15	16	17
18	19	20	21	22	23	24
25	26	27	28	29	30	31

November

S	M	T	W	T	F	S
1	2	3	4	5	6	7
8	9	10	11	12	13	14
15	16	17	18	19	20	21
22	23	24	25	26	27	28
29	30					

December

S	M	T	W	T	F	S
		1	2	3	4	5
6	7	8	9	10	11	12
13	14	15	16	17	18	19
20	21	22	23	24	25	26
27	28	29	30	31		

2021

January

S	M	T	W	T	F	S
					1	2
3	4	5	6	7	8	9
10	11	12	13	14	15	16
17	18	19	20	21	22	23
24	25	26	27	28	29	30
31						

February

S	M	T	W	T	F	S
	1	2	3	4	5	6
7	8	9	10	11	12	13
14	15	16	17	18	19	20
21	22	23	24	25	26	27
28						

March

S	M	T	W	T	F	S
	1	2	3	4	5	6
7	8	9	10	11	12	13
14	15	16	17	18	19	20
21	22	23	24	25	26	27
28	29	30	31			

April

S	M	T	W	T	F	S
				1	2	3
4	5	6	7	8	9	10
11	12	13	14	15	16	17
18	19	20	21	22	23	24
25	26	27	28	29	30	

May

S	M	T	W	T	F	S
						1
2	3	4	5	6	7	8
9	10	11	12	13	14	15
16	17	18	19	20	21	22
23	24	25	26	27	28	29
30	31					

June

S	M	T	W	T	F	S
		1	2	3	4	5
6	7	8	9	10	11	12
13	14	15	16	17	18	19
20	21	22	23	24	25	26
27	28	29	30			

July

S	M	T	W	T	F	S
				1	2	3
4	5	6	7	8	9	10
11	12	13	14	15	16	17
18	19	20	21	22	23	24
25	26	27	28	29	30	31

August

S	M	T	W	T	F	S
1	2	3	4	5	6	7
8	9	10	11	12	13	14
15	16	17	18	19	20	21
22	23	24	25	26	27	28
29	30	31				

September

S	M	T	W	T	F	S
			1	2	3	4
5	6	7	8	9	10	11
12	13	14	15	16	17	18
19	20	21	22	23	24	25
26	27	28	29	30		

October

S	M	T	W	T	F	S
					1	2
3	4	5	6	7	8	9
10	11	12	13	14	15	16
17	18	19	20	21	22	23
24	25	26	27	28	29	30
31						

November

S	M	T	W	T	F	S
	1	2	3	4	5	6
7	8	9	10	11	12	13
14	15	16	17	18	19	20
21	22	23	24	25	26	27
28	29	30				

December

S	M	T	W	T	F	S
			1	2	3	4
5	6	7	8	9	10	11
12	13	14	15	16	17	18
19	20	21	22	23	24	25
26	27	28	29	30	31	

DOGGY LANGUAGE

There's an entire language devoted to dogs; this language is known as Doggo Lingo. It's how your dog speaks and thinks. It's a fun, positive celebration of dogs.

Doggo	Doggos come in a variety of sizes ranked by the size of their bork (bark). They range from the tiny yapper to a diminutive pupper, an average-sized doggo, and the biggest woofers and boofers.
Longboi	A long-bodied dog such as a greyhound.
Floofer/Fluffer	A very fluffy dog such as a Samoyed or Pomeranian.
Thicc boi	A chubby dog – more to love.
Smol boi	A little yapper.
Woofer	A big dog.
Loaf	A dog, slightly overweight, which resembles a loaf of bread.
Pupper	A puppy.
Heckin' bamboozled	Sometimes you bamboozle the dog, sometimes the dog bamboozles you. Heck.
Do me a frighten	When a doggo is worried , scared or confused, potentially in the presence of borks or woofers.
Doin' me a	Having an action performed on oneself.
Bamboozle	A deceiving trick.
Awoo!	Howling.
Hooman	A human being.

DOGGY LANGUAGE

Blep/Blop	When your pupper is tired and his tongue hangs out just a little bit.
Mlem	Doing a lick. Not to be confused with a gentle blop.
Bork	Barking his little head off.
Boof	Not quite a bork, not quite a sneeze; it's the small huffy sound of a dog who's getting ready to bork..
Maximum borkdrive	This is otherwise known as the zoomies, when your doggo is going so fast they're just a blur.
Chimken	Chicken.
Fren	Friend
Henlo	Hello
Snoot	The nose always knows, and the snoot was made for booping.
Boop!	Touching your pet on the nose. Frequently accompanied by saying 'boop!'

Me and the hooman and the new fren went for a walk. And we saw other woofers and I jumped into a mud puddle. Awoo!

About My Dog

Dog's Name: ....

Date of Birth: ....

Breed: ....

Colour: ....

Gender: ....

Adoption Date: ....

Weight: ....

Breeder: ....

Microchip No: ....

Registration No: ....

Rabies: ....

Neutered/Speyed: ....

JANUARY

I REALLY LOVE THE SOUND OF MY DOG SNORING

JANUARY 2020

Sun	Mon	Tue	Wed	Thu	Fri	Sat
29	30	31	1	2	3	4
5	6	7	8	9	10	11
12	13	14	15	16	17	18
19	20	21	22	23	24	25
26	27	28	29	30	31	1

Notes:

January Photo

Wednesday

January 1st, 2020

6 am	
7	
8	
9	
10	
11	
12 pm	
1	
2	
3	
4	
5	
6	
7	
8	

PRIORITIES

TO DO

NOTES:

Thursday

January 2nd, 2020

6 am	
7	
8	
9	
10	
11	
12 pm	
1	
2	
3	
4	
5	
6	
7	
8	

PRIORITIES

TO DO

NOTES:

Friday

January 3rd, 2020

6 am	
7	
8	
9	
10	
11	
12 pm	
1	
2	
3	
4	
5	
6	
7	
8	

PRIORITIES

TO DO

NOTES:

Saturday

January 4th, 2020

6 am	
7	
8	
9	
10	
11	
12 pm	
1	
2	
3	
4	
5	
6	
7	
8	

PRIORITIES

TO DO

NOTES:

Sunday

January 5th, 2020

6 am	
7	
8	
9	
10	
11	
12 pm	
1	
2	
3	
4	
5	
6	
7	
8	

PRIORITIES

TO DO

NOTES:

Monday

January 6th, 2020

6 am	
7	
8	
9	
10	
11	
12 pm	
1	
2	
3	
4	
5	
6	
7	
8	

NOTES:

PRIORITIES

TO DO

Tuesday

January 7th, 2020

6 am	
7	
8	
9	
10	
11	
12 pm	
1	
2	
3	
4	
5	
6	
7	
8	

PRIORITIES

TO DO

NOTES:

Wednesday

January 8th, 2020

6 am	
7	
8	
9	
10	
11	
12 pm	
1	
2	
3	
4	
5	
6	
7	
8	

PRIORITIES

TO DO

NOTES:

Thursday

January 9th, 2020

6 am	
7	
8	
9	
10	
11	
12 pm	
1	
2	
3	
4	
5	
6	
7	
8	

PRIORITIES

TO DO

NOTES:

Friday

January 10th, 2020

6 am	
7	
8	
9	
10	
11	
12 pm	
1	
2	
3	
4	
5	
6	
7	
8	

PRIORITIES

TO DO

NOTES:

Saturday

January 11th, 2020

6 am	
7	
8	
9	
10	
11	
12 pm	
1	
2	
3	
4	
5	
6	
7	
8	

PRIORITIES

TO DO

NOTES:

Sunday

January 12th, 2020

6 am	
7	
8	
9	
10	
11	
12 pm	
1	
2	
3	
4	
5	
6	
7	
8	

PRIORITIES

TO DO

NOTES:

Monday

January 13th, 2020

6 am	
7	
8	
9	
10	
11	
12 pm	
1	
2	
3	
4	
5	
6	
7	
8	

PRIORITIES

TO DO

NOTES:

Tuesday

January 14th, 2020

6 am	
7	
8	
9	
10	
11	
12 pm	
1	
2	
3	
4	
5	
6	
7	
8	

PRIORITIES

TO DO

NOTES:

Easy Doggie Donuts

Ingredients:
1 cup flour
1 cup oats
1/3 cup coconut oil
1/2 cup peanut Butter
2 Eggs

For the topping:
Greek Yogurt
Bacon Bits

Directions:

Preheat your oven to 375 degrees. Spray a donut pan with cooking spray and set aside.

In a large bowl, combine all ingredients (except yogurt and bacon bits). You can mix with a spoon or use your hands (super fun for kids!). Mix until a dough forms. Use your hands to press the dough into the donut pan. Fill each donut cavity and press firmly to ensure everything sticks together (it won't rise, so you should make sure each space is tightly packed).

Bake in your preheated oven at 375 degrees for approximately 14 mins or until cooked completely.

Allow to cool, then carefully remove the donuts from the pan. Now you're ready to decorate them!

Set out a small bowl of plan Greek yogurt and another of bacon bits. Dip each donut carefully in the yogurt, then sprinkle with bacon bits.

Place your finished donuts in the freezer for a few moments to harden the yogurt. My dogs like to eat them straight from the freezer, but you can also store in the refrigerator. Just keep in mind that the yogurt may get a little sticky.

Wednesday

January 15th, 2020

6 am	
7	
8	
9	
10	
11	
12 pm	
1	
2	
3	
4	
5	
6	
7	
8	

PRIORITIES

TO DO

NOTES:

Thursday

January 16th, 2020

6 am	
7	
8	
9	
10	
11	
12 pm	
1	
2	
3	
4	
5	
6	
7	
8	

PRIORITIES

TO DO

NOTES:

Friday

January 17th, 2020

6 am	
7	
8	
9	
10	
11	
12 pm	
1	
2	
3	
4	
5	
6	
7	
8	

PRIORITIES

TO DO

NOTES:

Saturday

January 18th, 2020

6 am	
7	
8	
9	
10	
11	
12 pm	
1	
2	
3	
4	
5	
6	
7	
8	

PRIORITIES

TO DO

NOTES:

Sunday

January 19th, 2020

6 am	
7	
8	
9	
10	
11	
12 pm	
1	
2	
3	
4	
5	
6	
7	
8	

PRIORITIES

TO DO

NOTES:

Monday

January 20th, 2020

6 am	
7	
8	
9	
10	
11	
12 pm	
1	
2	
3	
4	
5	
6	
7	
8	

PRIORITIES

TO DO

NOTES:

Tuesday

January 21st, 2020

6 am	
7	
8	
9	
10	
11	
12 pm	
1	
2	
3	
4	
5	
6	
7	
8	

PRIORITIES

TO DO

NOTES:

Wednesday

January 22nd, 2020

6 am	
7	
8	
9	
10	
11	
12 pm	
1	
2	
3	
4	
5	
6	
7	
8	

PRIORITIES

TO DO

NOTES:

Thursday

January 23rd, 2020

6 am	
7	
8	
9	
10	
11	
12 pm	
1	
2	
3	
4	
5	
6	
7	
8	

PRIORITIES

TO DO

NOTES:

Friday

January 24th, 2020

6 am	
7	
8	
9	
10	
11	
12 pm	
1	
2	
3	
4	
5	
6	
7	
8	

PRIORITIES

TO DO

NOTES:

Saturday

January 25th, 2020

6 am	
7	
8	
9	
10	
11	
12 pm	
1	
2	
3	
4	
5	
6	
7	
8	

PRIORITIES

TO DO

NOTES:

Sunday

January 26th, 2020

6 am	
7	
8	
9	
10	
11	
12 pm	
1	
2	
3	
4	
5	
6	
7	
8	

PRIORITIES

TO DO

NOTES:

Monday

January 27th, 2020

6 am	
7	
8	
9	
10	
11	
12 pm	
1	
2	
3	
4	
5	
6	
7	
8	

PRIORITIES

TO DO

NOTES:

Tuesday

January 28th, 2020

6 am	
7	
8	
9	
10	
11	
12 pm	
1	
2	
3	
4	
5	
6	
7	
8	

PRIORITIES

TO DO

NOTES:

Wednesday

January 29th, 2020

6 am	
7	
8	
9	
10	
11	
12 pm	
1	
2	
3	
4	
5	
6	
7	
8	

PRIORITIES

TO DO

NOTES:

Thursday

January 30th, 2020

6 am	
7	
8	
9	
10	
11	
12 pm	
1	
2	
3	
4	
5	
6	
7	
8	

PRIORITIES

TO DO

NOTES:

Friday

January 31st, 2020

6 am	
7	
8	
9	
10	
11	
12 pm	
1	
2	
3	
4	
5	
6	
7	
8	

PRIORITIES

TO DO

NOTES:

Notes...

CAN'T SLEEP...

THINKING ABOUT... PEANUT BUTTER

FEBRUARY
DOGS' LIVES ARE TOO SHORT. IT'S THEIR ONLY FAULT

FEBRUARY 2020

Sun	Mon	Tue	Wed	Thu	Fri	Sat
26	27	28	29	30	31	1
2	3	4	5	6	7	8
9	10	11	12	13	14	15
16	17	18	19	20	21	22
23	24	25	26	27	28	29

Notes:

February Photo

A new week is upon us....
Or so the hooman tells me.
Hooman time constructs do me a bamboozle. I prefer to break it down into snoozes, non snoozes and.......

MAXIMUM BORKDRIVE

Saturday

February 1st, 2020

6 am	
7	
8	
9	
10	
11	
12 pm	
1	
2	
3	
4	
5	
6	
7	
8	

PRIORITIES

TO DO

NOTES:

Sunday

February 2nd, 2020

6 am	
7	
8	
9	
10	
11	
12 pm	
1	
2	
3	
4	
5	
6	
7	
8	

PRIORITIES

TO DO

NOTES:

Monday

February 3rd, 2020

6 am	
7	
8	
9	
10	
11	
12 pm	
1	
2	
3	
4	
5	
6	
7	
8	

PRIORITIES

TO DO

NOTES:

Tuesday

February 4th, 2020

6 am	
7	
8	
9	
10	
11	
12 pm	
1	
2	
3	
4	
5	
6	
7	
8	

PRIORITIES

TO DO

NOTES:

Wednesday

February 5th, 2020

6 am	
7	
8	
9	
10	
11	
12 pm	
1	
2	
3	
4	
5	
6	
7	
8	

PRIORITIES

TO DO

NOTES:

Thursday

February 6th, 2020

6 am	
7	
8	
9	
10	
11	
12 pm	
1	
2	
3	
4	
5	
6	
7	
8	

PRIORITIES

TO DO

NOTES:

Friday

February 7th, 2020

6 am	
7	
8	
9	
10	
11	
12 pm	
1	
2	
3	
4	
5	
6	
7	
8	

PRIORITIES

TO DO

NOTES:

Saturday

February 8th, 2020

6 am	
7	
8	
9	
10	
11	
12 pm	
1	
2	
3	
4	
5	
6	
7	
8	

PRIORITIES

TO DO

NOTES:

Sunday

February 9th, 2020

6 am	
7	
8	
9	
10	
11	
12 pm	
1	
2	
3	
4	
5	
6	
7	
8	

PRIORITIES

TO DO

NOTES:

Monday

February 10th, 2020

6 am	
7	
8	
9	
10	
11	
12 pm	
1	
2	
3	
4	
5	
6	
7	
8	

PRIORITIES

TO DO

NOTES:

Tuesday

February 11th, 2020

6 am	
7	
8	
9	
10	
11	
12 pm	
1	
2	
3	
4	
5	
6	
7	
8	

PRIORITIES

TO DO

NOTES:

Wednesday

February 12th, 2020

6 am	
7	
8	
9	
10	
11	
12 pm	
1	
2	
3	
4	
5	
6	
7	
8	

PRIORITIES

TO DO

NOTES:

Thursday

February 13th, 2020

6 am	
7	
8	
9	
10	
11	
12 pm	
1	
2	
3	
4	
5	
6	
7	
8	

PRIORITIES

TO DO

NOTES:

Friday

February 14th, 2020

6 am	
7	
8	
9	
10	
11	
12 pm	
1	
2	
3	
4	
5	
6	
7	
8	

PRIORITIES

TO DO

NOTES:

Bacon & Peanut Butter Glaze

Ingredients:

Dog biscuits:

- 1 cup pumpkin
- 1/2 cup peanut butter
- 2 eggs
- 1/4 cup oil
- 2 1/2 cups whole wheat flour
- 1 teaspoon baking soda

Glaze:

- 2 tablespoons bacon grease, coconut oil, chicken fat, or any other fat that will solidify at room temperature, melted
- 1/4 cup smooth peanut butter

Instructions:

Preheat oven to 350 degrees.

Combine pumpkin, peanut butter, eggs, and oil in a bowl. Add in baking soda and whole wheat flour. Stir until a stiff dough forms. Knead dough or mix just until flour is incorporated.

Roll out dough with a rolling pin and use a cookie cutter to cut out dog bone shapes, or just bake into little circles like cookies. Bake for 15 minutes.

Whisk the bacon grease and peanut butter until very smooth. Drizzle over the treats and cool till glaze hardens (it does best in the fridge or freezer).

Please check with your vet or use an alternative type of oil if you are concerned about bacon grease.

Saturday

February 15th, 2020

6 am	
7	
8	
9	
10	
11	
12 pm	
1	
2	
3	
4	
5	
6	
7	
8	

PRIORITIES

TO DO

NOTES:

Sunday

February 16th, 2020

6 am	
7	
8	
9	
10	
11	
12 pm	
1	
2	
3	
4	
5	
6	
7	
8	

PRIORITIES

TO DO

NOTES:

Monday

February 17th, 2020

6 am	
7	
8	
9	
10	
11	
12 pm	
1	
2	
3	
4	
5	
6	
7	
8	

PRIORITIES

TO DO

NOTES:

Tuesday

February 18th, 2020

6 am	
7	
8	
9	
10	
11	
12 pm	
1	
2	
3	
4	
5	
6	
7	
8	

PRIORITIES

TO DO

NOTES:

Wednesday

February 19th, 2020

6 am	
7	
8	
9	
10	
11	
12 pm	
1	
2	
3	
4	
5	
6	
7	
8	

PRIORITIES

TO DO

NOTES:

Thursday

February 20th, 2020

6 am	
7	
8	
9	
10	
11	
12 pm	
1	
2	
3	
4	
5	
6	
7	
8	

PRIORITIES

TO DO

NOTES:

Friday

February 21st, 2020

6 am	
7	
8	
9	
10	
11	
12 pm	
1	
2	
3	
4	
5	
6	
7	
8	

PRIORITIES

TO DO

NOTES:

Saturday

February 22nd, 2020

6 am	
7	
8	
9	
10	
11	
12 pm	
1	
2	
3	
4	
5	
6	
7	
8	

PRIORITIES

TO DO

NOTES:

Sunday

February 23rd, 2020

6 am	
7	
8	
9	
10	
11	
12 pm	
1	
2	
3	
4	
5	
6	
7	
8	

PRIORITIES

TO DO

NOTES:

Monday

February 24th, 2020

6 am	
7	
8	
9	
10	
11	
12 pm	
1	
2	
3	
4	
5	
6	
7	
8	

PRIORITIES

TO DO

NOTES:

Tuesday

February 25th, 2020

6 am	
7	
8	
9	
10	
11	
12 pm	
1	
2	
3	
4	
5	
6	
7	
8	

PRIORITIES

TO DO

NOTES:

Wednesday

February 26th, 2020

6 am	
7	
8	
9	
10	
11	
12 pm	
1	
2	
3	
4	
5	
6	
7	
8	

PRIORITIES

TO DO

NOTES:

Thursday

February 27th, 2020

6 am	
7	
8	
9	
10	
11	
12 pm	
1	
2	
3	
4	
5	
6	
7	
8	

PRIORITIES

TO DO

NOTES:

Friday

February 28th, 2020

6 am	
7	
8	
9	
10	
11	
12 pm	
1	
2	
3	
4	
5	
6	
7	
8	

PRIORITIES

TO DO

NOTES:

Saturday

February 29th, 2020

6 am	
7	
8	
9	
10	
11	
12 pm	
1	
2	
3	
4	
5	
6	
7	
8	

PRIORITIES

TO DO

NOTES:

Notes...

Early morning
walks are for
practicing fancy
trots and
prances!

MARCH

DOGS' ARE NOT
OUR WHOLE LIFE,
BUT THEY MAKE
OUR LIFE WHOLE

MARCH 2020

Sun	Mon	Tue	Wed	Thu	Fri	Sat
1	2	3	4	5	6	7
8	9	10	11	12	13	14
15	16	17	18	19	20	21
22	23	24	25	26	27	28
29	30	31	1	2	3	4

Notes:

March Photo

Sometimes, I grrbork at the sky... in case anybody is listening.
You ever wake up in the middle of the night and think...why?
I NEED CHIMKIN!

Sunday

March 1st, 2020

6 am	
7	
8	
9	
10	
11	
12 pm	
1	
2	
3	
4	
5	
6	
7	
8	

PRIORITIES

TO DO

NOTES:

Monday

March 2nd, 2020

6 am	
7	
8	
9	
10	
11	
12 pm	
1	
2	
3	
4	
5	
6	
7	
8	

PRIORITIES

TO DO

NOTES:

Tuesday

March 3rd, 2020

6 am	
7	
8	
9	
10	
11	
12 pm	
1	
2	
3	
4	
5	
6	
7	
8	

PRIORITIES

TO DO

NOTES:

Wednesday

March 4th, 2020

6 am	
7	
8	
9	
10	
11	
12 pm	
1	
2	
3	
4	
5	
6	
7	
8	

PRIORITIES

TO DO

NOTES:

Thursday

March 5th, 2020

6 am	
7	
8	
9	
10	
11	
12 pm	
1	
2	
3	
4	
5	
6	
7	
8	

PRIORITIES

TO DO

NOTES:

Friday

March 6th, 2020

6 am	
7	
8	
9	
10	
11	
12 pm	
1	
2	
3	
4	
5	
6	
7	
8	

PRIORITIES

TO DO

NOTES:

Saturday

March 7th, 2020

6 am	
7	
8	
9	
10	
11	
12 pm	
1	
2	
3	
4	
5	
6	
7	
8	

PRIORITIES

TO DO

NOTES:

Sunday

March 8th, 2020

6 am	
7	
8	
9	
10	
11	
12 pm	
1	
2	
3	
4	
5	
6	
7	
8	

PRIORITIES

TO DO

NOTES:

Monday

March 9th, 2020

6 am	
7	
8	
9	
10	
11	
12 pm	
1	
2	
3	
4	
5	
6	
7	
8	

PRIORITIES

TO DO

NOTES:

Tuesday

March 10th, 2020

6 am	
7	
8	
9	
10	
11	
12 pm	
1	
2	
3	
4	
5	
6	
7	
8	

PRIORITIES

TO DO

NOTES:

Wednesday

March 11th, 2020

6 am	
7	
8	
9	
10	
11	
12 pm	
1	
2	
3	
4	
5	
6	
7	
8	

PRIORITIES

TO DO

NOTES:

Thursday

March 12th, 2020

6 am	
7	
8	
9	
10	
11	
12 pm	
1	
2	
3	
4	
5	
6	
7	
8	

PRIORITIES

TO DO

NOTES:

Friday

March 13th, 2020

6 am	
7	
8	
9	
10	
11	
12 pm	
1	
2	
3	
4	
5	
6	
7	
8	

PRIORITIES

TO DO

NOTES:

Saturday

March 14th, 2020

6 am	
7	
8	
9	
10	
11	
12 pm	
1	
2	
3	
4	
5	
6	
7	
8	

PRIORITIES

TO DO

NOTES:

Spinach, Carrot & Zucchini Treats

Ingredients:

- 1 cup pumpkin puree
- 1/4 cup peanut butter
- 2 large eggs
- 1/2 cup old fashioned oats
- 3 cups whole wheat flour, or more, as needed
- 1 carrot, peeled and shredded
- 1 zucchini, shredded
- 1 cup baby spinach, chopped

Instructions:

Preheat oven to 350 degrees F. Line a baking sheet with parchment paper or a silicone baking mat; set aside.

In the bowl of an electric mixer fitted with the paddle attachment, beat pumpkin puree, peanut butter and eggs on medium-high until well combined, about 1-2 minutes.

Gradually add old fashioned oats and 2 1/2 cups flour at low speed, beating just until incorporated. Add an additional 1/4 cup flour at a time just until the dough is no longer sticky. Add carrot, zucchini and spinach, beating just until incorporated.

Working on a lightly floured surface, knead the dough 3-4 times until it comes together. Using a rolling pin, roll the dough to 1/4-inch thickness. Using cookie cutters, cut out desired shapes and place onto the prepared baking sheet.

Place into oven and bake until the edges are golden brown, about 20-25 minutes. Let cool completely.

Sunday

March 15th, 2020

6 am	
7	
8	
9	
10	
11	
12 pm	
1	
2	
3	
4	
5	
6	
7	
8	

PRIORITIES

TO DO

NOTES:

Monday

March 16th, 2020

6 am	
7	
8	
9	
10	
11	
12 pm	
1	
2	
3	
4	
5	
6	
7	
8	

PRIORITIES

TO DO

NOTES:

Tuesday

March 17th, 2020

6 am	
7	
8	
9	
10	
11	
12 pm	
1	
2	
3	
4	
5	
6	
7	
8	

PRIORITIES

TO DO

NOTES:

Wednesday

March 18th, 2020

6 am	
7	
8	
9	
10	
11	
12 pm	
1	
2	
3	
4	
5	
6	
7	
8	

PRIORITIES

TO DO

NOTES:

Thursday

March 19th, 2020

6 am	
7	
8	
9	
10	
11	
12 pm	
1	
2	
3	
4	
5	
6	
7	
8	

PRIORITIES

TO DO

NOTES:

Friday

March 20th, 2020

6 am	
7	
8	
9	
10	
11	
12 pm	
1	
2	
3	
4	
5	
6	
7	
8	

PRIORITIES

TO DO

NOTES:

Saturday

March 21st, 2020

6 am	
7	
8	
9	
10	
11	
12 pm	
1	
2	
3	
4	
5	
6	
7	
8	

PRIORITIES

TO DO

NOTES:

Sunday

March 22nd, 2020

6 am	
7	
8	
9	
10	
11	
12 pm	
1	
2	
3	
4	
5	
6	
7	
8	

PRIORITIES

TO DO

NOTES:

Monday

March 23rd, 2020

6 am	
7	
8	
9	
10	
11	
12 pm	
1	
2	
3	
4	
5	
6	
7	
8	

PRIORITIES

TO DO

NOTES:

Tuesday

March 24th, 2020

6 am	
7	
8	
9	
10	
11	
12 pm	
1	
2	
3	
4	
5	
6	
7	
8	

PRIORITIES

TO DO

NOTES:

Wednesday

March 25th, 2020

6 am	
7	
8	
9	
10	
11	
12 pm	
1	
2	
3	
4	
5	
6	
7	
8	

PRIORITIES

TO DO

NOTES:

Thursday

March 26th, 2020

6 am	
7	
8	
9	
10	
11	
12 pm	
1	
2	
3	
4	
5	
6	
7	
8	

NOTES:

PRIORITIES

TO DO

Friday

March 27th, 2020

6 am	
7	
8	
9	
10	
11	
12 pm	
1	
2	
3	
4	
5	
6	
7	
8	

PRIORITIES

TO DO

NOTES:

Saturday

March 28th, 2020

6 am	
7	
8	
9	
10	
11	
12 pm	
1	
2	
3	
4	
5	
6	
7	
8	

PRIORITIES

TO DO

NOTES:

Sunday

March 29th, 2020

6 am	
7	
8	
9	
10	
11	
12 pm	
1	
2	
3	
4	
5	
6	
7	
8	

PRIORITIES

TO DO

NOTES:

Monday

March 30th, 2020

6 am	
7	
8	
9	
10	
11	
12 pm	
1	
2	
3	
4	
5	
6	
7	
8	

PRIORITIES

TO DO

NOTES:

Tuesday

March 31st, 2020

6 am	
7	
8	
9	
10	
11	
12 pm	
1	
2	
3	
4	
5	
6	
7	
8	

PRIORITIES

TO DO

NOTES:

Notes...

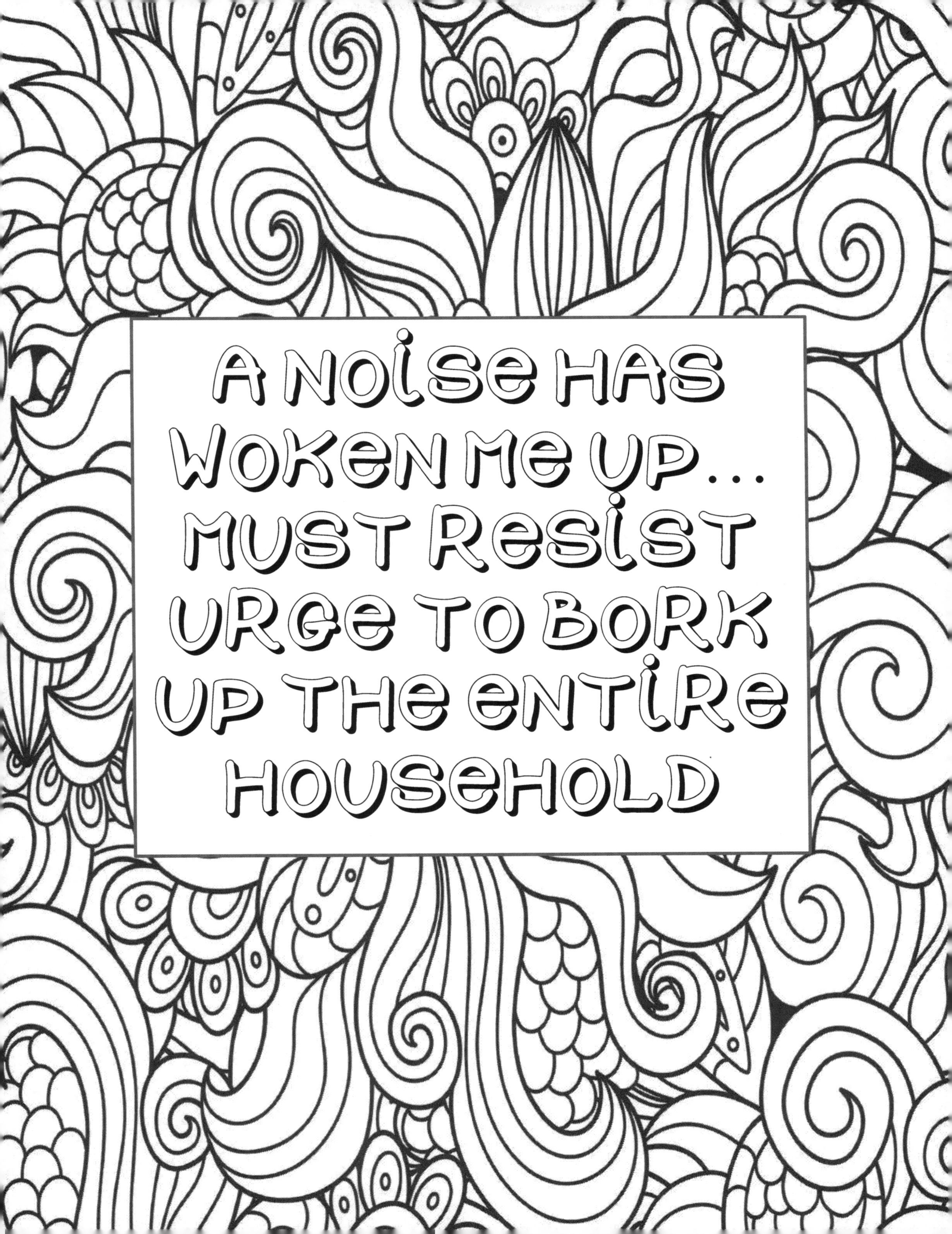
A NOISE HAS
WOKEN ME UP...
MUST RESIST
URGE TO BORK
UP THE ENTIRE
HOUSEHOLD

APRIL

ANYBODY WHO DOESN'T KNOW WHAT SOAP TASTES LIKE HAS NEVER WASHED A DOG

APRIL 2020

Sun	Mon	Tue	Wed	Thu	Fri	Sat
29	30	31	1	2	3	4
5	6	7	8	9	10	11
12	13	14	15	16	17	18
19	20	21	22	23	24	25
26	27	28	29	30	1	2

Notes:

April Photo

Guys, I just had a morning walk. Some big doggo borked at me and I almost caught Bruce, the lizard.
LIFE IS GOOD!

Wednesday

April 1st, 2020

6 am	
7	
8	
9	
10	
11	
12 pm	
1	
2	
3	
4	
5	
6	
7	
8	

PRIORITIES

TO DO

NOTES:

Thursday

April 2nd, 2020

6 am	
7	
8	
9	
10	
11	
12 pm	
1	
2	
3	
4	
5	
6	
7	
8	

PRIORITIES

TO DO

NOTES:

Friday

April 3rd, 2020

6 am	
7	
8	
9	
10	
11	
12 pm	
1	
2	
3	
4	
5	
6	
7	
8	

PRIORITIES

TO DO

NOTES:

Saturday

April 4th, 2020

6 am	
7	
8	
9	
10	
11	
12 pm	
1	
2	
3	
4	
5	
6	
7	
8	

PRIORITIES

TO DO

NOTES:

Sunday

April 5th, 2020

6 am	
7	
8	
9	
10	
11	
12 pm	
1	
2	
3	
4	
5	
6	
7	
8	

PRIORITIES

TO DO

NOTES:

Monday

April 6th, 2020

6 am	
7	
8	
9	
10	
11	
12 pm	
1	
2	
3	
4	
5	
6	
7	
8	

PRIORITIES

TO DO

NOTES:

Tuesday

April 7th, 2020

6 am	
7	
8	
9	
10	
11	
12 pm	
1	
2	
3	
4	
5	
6	
7	
8	

PRIORITIES

TO DO

NOTES:

Wednesday

April 8th, 2020

6 am	
7	
8	
9	
10	
11	
12 pm	
1	
2	
3	
4	
5	
6	
7	
8	

PRIORITIES

TO DO

NOTES:

Thursday

April 9th, 2020

6 am	
7	
8	
9	
10	
11	
12 pm	
1	
2	
3	
4	
5	
6	
7	
8	

PRIORITIES

TO DO

NOTES:

Friday

April 10th, 2020

6 am	
7	
8	
9	
10	
11	
12 pm	
1	
2	
3	
4	
5	
6	
7	
8	

PRIORITIES

TO DO

NOTES:

Saturday

April 11th, 2020

6 am	
7	
8	
9	
10	
11	
12 pm	
1	
2	
3	
4	
5	
6	
7	
8	

PRIORITIES

TO DO

NOTES:

Sunday

April 12th, 2020

6 am	
7	
8	
9	
10	
11	
12 pm	
1	
2	
3	
4	
5	
6	
7	
8	

PRIORITIES

TO DO

NOTES:

Monday

April 13th, 2020

6 am	
7	
8	
9	
10	
11	
12 pm	
1	
2	
3	
4	
5	
6	
7	
8	

PRIORITIES

TO DO

NOTES:

Tuesday

April 14th, 2020

6 am	
7	
8	
9	
10	
11	
12 pm	
1	
2	
3	
4	
5	
6	
7	
8	

PRIORITIES

TO DO

NOTES:

Bacon Cheddar Treats

Ingredients:

- 1 ½ cups rolled oats
- ½ cup shredded cheddar cheese
- 4 strips bacon, cooked and crumbled
- 2 eggs

Instructions:

Preheat oven to 350 degrees Fahrenheit.
Add oats, cheese, and bacon to the bowl of a food processor and process until ingredients reach a crumb-like consistency.
Add two eggs to food processor and process until mixture resembles a sticky dough.
Sprinkle flour or finely ground oats onto a wood cutting board and roll out dough to about ¼-inch thick. Using a cookie cutter, cut out dough into desired shape.
Transfer dog treats to a parchment-lined baking sheet and cook for 20 minutes.
Cool treats completely and store in an airtight glass or plastic container.

Wednesday

April 15th, 2020

6 am	
7	
8	
9	
10	
11	
12 pm	
1	
2	
3	
4	
5	
6	
7	
8	

PRIORITIES

TO DO

NOTES:

Thursday

April 16th, 2020

6 am	
7	
8	
9	
10	
11	
12 pm	
1	
2	
3	
4	
5	
6	
7	
8	

PRIORITIES

TO DO

NOTES:

Friday

April 17th, 2020

6 am	
7	
8	
9	
10	
11	
12 pm	
1	
2	
3	
4	
5	
6	
7	
8	

PRIORITIES

TO DO

NOTES:

Saturday

April 18th, 2020

6 am	
7	
8	
9	
10	
11	
12 pm	
1	
2	
3	
4	
5	
6	
7	
8	

PRIORITIES

TO DO

NOTES:

Sunday

April 19th, 2020

6 am	
7	
8	
9	
10	
11	
12 pm	
1	
2	
3	
4	
5	
6	
7	
8	

PRIORITIES

TO DO

NOTES:

Monday

April 20th, 2020

6 am	
7	
8	
9	
10	
11	
12 pm	
1	
2	
3	
4	
5	
6	
7	
8	

PRIORITIES

TO DO

NOTES:

Tuesday

April 21st, 2020

6 am	
7	
8	
9	
10	
11	
12 pm	
1	
2	
3	
4	
5	
6	
7	
8	

PRIORITIES

TO DO

NOTES:

Wednesday

April 22nd, 2020

6 am	
7	
8	
9	
10	
11	
12 pm	
1	
2	
3	
4	
5	
6	
7	
8	

PRIORITIES

TO DO

NOTES:

Thursday

April 23rd, 2020

6 am	
7	
8	
9	
10	
11	
12 pm	
1	
2	
3	
4	
5	
6	
7	
8	

PRIORITIES

TO DO

NOTES:

Friday

April 24th, 2020

6 am	
7	
8	
9	
10	
11	
12 pm	
1	
2	
3	
4	
5	
6	
7	
8	

PRIORITIES

TO DO

NOTES:

Saturday

April 25th, 2020

6 am	
7	
8	
9	
10	
11	
12 pm	
1	
2	
3	
4	
5	
6	
7	
8	

PRIORITIES

TO DO

NOTES:

Sunday

April 26th, 2020

6 am	
7	
8	
9	
10	
11	
12 pm	
1	
2	
3	
4	
5	
6	
7	
8	

PRIORITIES

TO DO

NOTES:

Monday

April 27th, 2020

6 am	
7	
8	
9	
10	
11	
12 pm	
1	
2	
3	
4	
5	
6	
7	
8	

PRIORITIES

TO DO

NOTES:

Tuesday

April 28th, 2020

6 am	
7	
8	
9	
10	
11	
12 pm	
1	
2	
3	
4	
5	
6	
7	
8	

PRIORITIES

TO DO

NOTES:

Wednesday

April 29th, 2020

6 am	
7	
8	
9	
10	
11	
12 pm	
1	
2	
3	
4	
5	
6	
7	
8	

PRIORITIES

TO DO

NOTES:

Thursday

April 30th, 2020

6 am	
7	
8	
9	
10	
11	
12 pm	
1	
2	
3	
4	
5	
6	
7	
8	

PRIORITIES

TO DO

NOTES:

Notes...

MY ZOOMIES ARE IMPROVING... I KNOW THIS BECAUSE THE PHOTOS ARE GETTING MORE BLURRY!

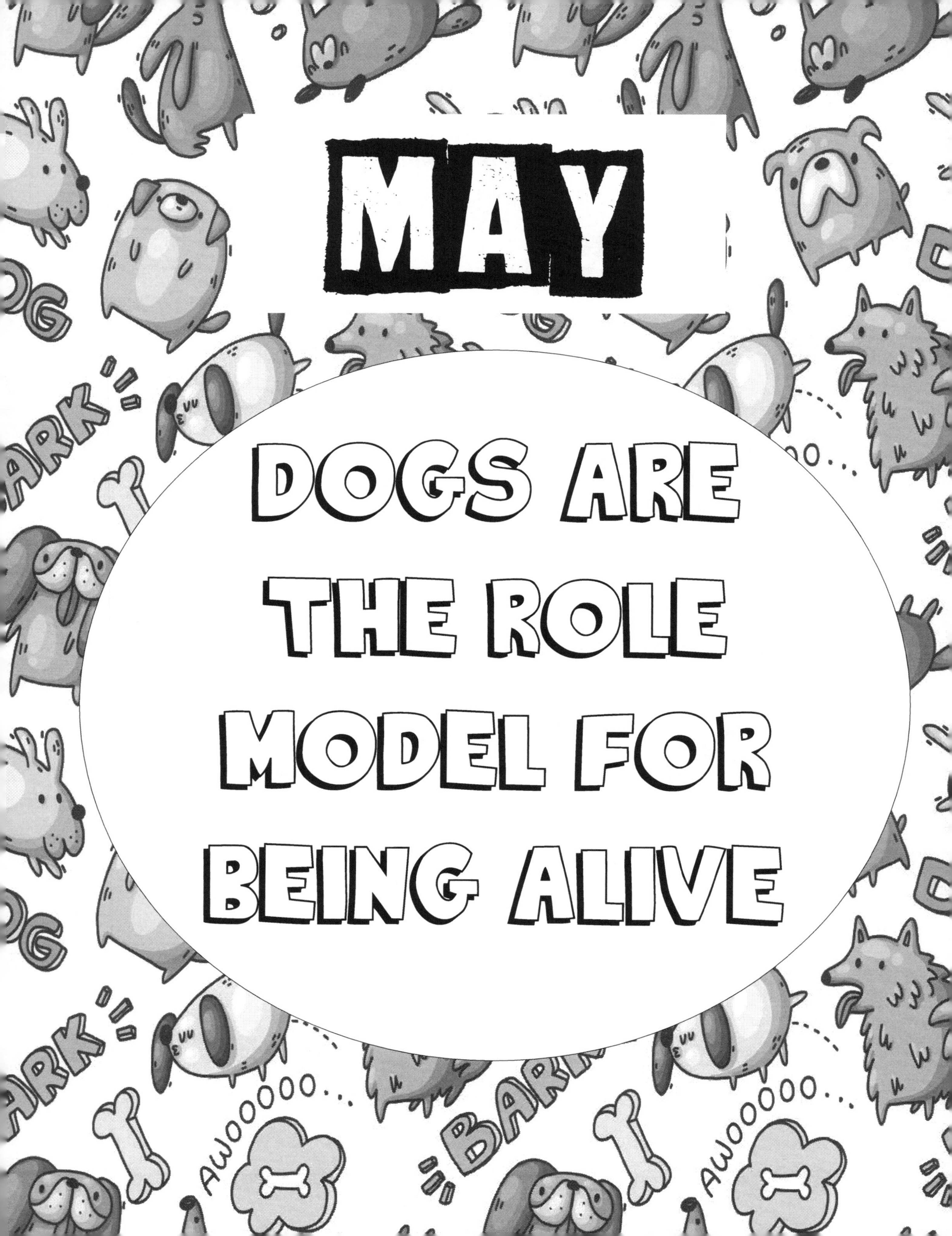

MAY

DOGS ARE THE ROLE MODEL FOR BEING ALIVE

MAY 2020

Sun	Mon	Tue	Wed	Thu	Fri	Sat
26	27	28	29	30	1	2
3	4	5	6	7	8	9
10	11	12	13	14	15	16
17	18	19	20	21	22	23
24	25	26	27	28	29	30
31	1	2	3	4	5	6

Notes:

May Photo

Human gave me an extra long hug and direct eye contact. These are heckin' signals. We're on the same page.

I FEEL CHIMKIN COMING!

Friday

May 1st, 2020

6 am	
7	
8	
9	
10	
11	
12 pm	
1	
2	
3	
4	
5	
6	
7	
8	

PRIORITIES

TO DO

NOTES:

Saturday

May 2nd, 2020

6 am	
7	
8	
9	
10	
11	
12 pm	
1	
2	
3	
4	
5	
6	
7	
8	

PRIORITIES

TO DO

NOTES:

Sunday

May 3rd, 2020

6 am	
7	
8	
9	
10	
11	
12 pm	
1	
2	
3	
4	
5	
6	
7	
8	

PRIORITIES

TO DO

NOTES:

Monday

May 4th, 2020

6 am	
7	
8	
9	
10	
11	
12 pm	
1	
2	
3	
4	
5	
6	
7	
8	

PRIORITIES

TO DO

NOTES:

Tuesday

May 5th, 2020

6 am	
7	
8	
9	
10	
11	
12 pm	
1	
2	
3	
4	
5	
6	
7	
8	

PRIORITIES

TO DO

NOTES:

Wednesday

May 6th, 2020

6 am	
7	
8	
9	
10	
11	
12 pm	
1	
2	
3	
4	
5	
6	
7	
8	

PRIORITIES

TO DO

NOTES:

Thursday

May 7th, 2020

6 am	
7	
8	
9	
10	
11	
12 pm	
1	
2	
3	
4	
5	
6	
7	
8	

PRIORITIES

TO DO

NOTES:

Friday

May 8th, 2020

6 am	
7	
8	
9	
10	
11	
12 pm	
1	
2	
3	
4	
5	
6	
7	
8	

PRIORITIES

TO DO

NOTES:

Saturday

May 9th, 2020

6 am	
7	
8	
9	
10	
11	
12 pm	
1	
2	
3	
4	
5	
6	
7	
8	

NOTES:

PRIORITIES

TO DO

Sunday

May 10th, 2020

6 am	
7	
8	
9	
10	
11	
12 pm	
1	
2	
3	
4	
5	
6	
7	
8	

PRIORITIES

TO DO

NOTES:

Monday

May 11th, 2020

6 am	
7	
8	
9	
10	
11	
12 pm	
1	
2	
3	
4	
5	
6	
7	
8	

PRIORITIES

TO DO

NOTES:

Tuesday

May 12th, 2020

6 am	
7	
8	
9	
10	
11	
12 pm	
1	
2	
3	
4	
5	
6	
7	
8	

PRIORITIES

TO DO

NOTES:

Wednesday

May 13th, 2020

6 am	
7	
8	
9	
10	
11	
12 pm	
1	
2	
3	
4	
5	
6	
7	
8	

PRIORITIES

TO DO

NOTES:

Thursday

May 14th, 2020

6 am	
7	
8	
9	
10	
11	
12 pm	
1	
2	
3	
4	
5	
6	
7	
8	

PRIORITIES

TO DO

NOTES:

Chicken & Wild Rice Biscuits

Ingredients:

- Start off by boiling a piece of boneless chicken breast and making wild rice; then allowed them to cool. You can do this a day ahead and keep refrigerated until ready to use.
- Puree the chicken and rice with some chicken stock in a mini food processor or blender
- Add flour, salt, egg and pureed chicken and rice to a bowl and mix well; then roll out the dough on a lightly floured board until 1/2-inch thick.
- You can use any cookie cutter or glass to cut out the biscuits.
- Once you cut out the shapes, bake for about 30 minutes; then allow to harden.

Instructions:

Preheat oven to 350 degrees F.

Combine chicken, rice and chicken stock in a mini food processor or blender and pulse until a paste forms.

Add the flour, salt, egg and chicken paste into a bowl and mix well.

Sprinkle a little flour on a flat surface and knead dough until it's no longer sticky; then roll it out with a rolling pin about 1/2-inch thick.

Cut out shapes and place them on a parchment paper lined baking sheet.

Mine yielded 32 biscuits using a 3.5" cookie cutter.

Bake for 25-30 minutes until light brown. Remove from oven and allow to cool completely before serving.

Chicken & Wild Rice Biscuits

Keep these biscuits in an airtight container for up to one week. These biscuits can be stored in an airtight container in the freezer for up to 6 months. Allow to defrost completely (10-20 minutes) before serving.

Friday

May 15th, 2020

6 am	
7	
8	
9	
10	
11	
12 pm	
1	
2	
3	
4	
5	
6	
7	
8	

PRIORITIES

TO DO

NOTES:

Saturday

May 16th, 2020

6 am	
7	
8	
9	
10	
11	
12 pm	
1	
2	
3	
4	
5	
6	
7	
8	

PRIORITIES

TO DO

NOTES:

Sunday

May 17th, 2020

6 am	
7	
8	
9	
10	
11	
12 pm	
1	
2	
3	
4	
5	
6	
7	
8	

PRIORITIES

TO DO

NOTES:

Monday

May 18th, 2020

6 am	
7	
8	
9	
10	
11	
12 pm	
1	
2	
3	
4	
5	
6	
7	
8	

PRIORITIES

TO DO

NOTES:

Tuesday

May 19th, 2020

6 am	
7	
8	
9	
10	
11	
12 pm	
1	
2	
3	
4	
5	
6	
7	
8	

PRIORITIES

TO DO

NOTES:

Wednesday

May 20th, 2020

6 am	
7	
8	
9	
10	
11	
12 pm	
1	
2	
3	
4	
5	
6	
7	
8	

PRIORITIES

TO DO

NOTES:

Thursday

May 21st, 2020

6 am	
7	
8	
9	
10	
11	
12 pm	
1	
2	
3	
4	
5	
6	
7	
8	

NOTES:

PRIORITIES

TO DO

Friday

May 22nd, 2020

6 am	
7	
8	
9	
10	
11	
12 pm	
1	
2	
3	
4	
5	
6	
7	
8	

PRIORITIES

TO DO

NOTES:

Saturday

May 23rd, 2020

6 am	
7	
8	
9	
10	
11	
12 pm	
1	
2	
3	
4	
5	
6	
7	
8	

PRIORITIES

TO DO

NOTES:

Sunday

May 24th, 2020

6 am	
7	
8	
9	
10	
11	
12 pm	
1	
2	
3	
4	
5	
6	
7	
8	

PRIORITIES

TO DO

NOTES:

Monday

May 25th, 2020

6 am	
7	
8	
9	
10	
11	
12 pm	
1	
2	
3	
4	
5	
6	
7	
8	

PRIORITIES

TO DO

NOTES:

Tuesday

May 26th, 2020

6 am	
7	
8	
9	
10	
11	
12 pm	
1	
2	
3	
4	
5	
6	
7	
8	

PRIORITIES

TO DO

NOTES:

Wednesday

May 27th, 2020

6 am	
7	
8	
9	
10	
11	
12 pm	
1	
2	
3	
4	
5	
6	
7	
8	

PRIORITIES

TO DO

NOTES:

Thursday

May 28th, 2020

6 am	
7	
8	
9	
10	
11	
12 pm	
1	
2	
3	
4	
5	
6	
7	
8	

PRIORITIES

TO DO

NOTES:

Friday

May 29th, 2020

6 am	
7	
8	
9	
10	
11	
12 pm	
1	
2	
3	
4	
5	
6	
7	
8	

PRIORITIES

TO DO

NOTES:

Saturday

May 30th, 2020

6 am	
7	
8	
9	
10	
11	
12 pm	
1	
2	
3	
4	
5	
6	
7	
8	

PRIORITIES

TO DO

NOTES:

Sunday

May 31st, 2020

6 am	
7	
8	
9	
10	
11	
12 pm	
1	
2	
3	
4	
5	
6	
7	
8	

PRIORITIES

TO DO

NOTES:

Notes...

THE GARAGE HAS
OPENED...
THE HOOMAN IS HOME!!!
MAXIMUM BORKDRIVE...
I AM SO EXCITED.

JUNE
A DOG DOES
NOT THINK MUCH
ABOUT WHAT HE
IS DOING; HE
JUST DOES WHAT
FEELS RIGHT
BARK!!
AWOOOOO...

JUNE 2020

Sun	Mon	Tue	Wed	Thu	Fri	Sat
31	1	2	3	4	5	6
7	8	9	10	11	12	13
14	15	16	17	18	19	20
21	22	23	24	25	26	27
28	29	30	1	2	3	4

Notes:

June Photo

I have been programming my hooman. Every time they give me food, I bork. Eventually, every time I bork, they will give me food.
I WANT CHEESE!

Monday

June 1st, 2020

6 am	
7	
8	
9	
10	
11	
12 pm	
1	
2	
3	
4	
5	
6	
7	
8	

PRIORITIES

TO DO

NOTES:

Tuesday

June 2nd, 2020

6 am	
7	
8	
9	
10	
11	
12 pm	
1	
2	
3	
4	
5	
6	
7	
8	

PRIORITIES

TO DO

NOTES:

Wednesday

June 3rd, 2020

6 am	
7	
8	
9	
10	
11	
12 pm	
1	
2	
3	
4	
5	
6	
7	
8	

PRIORITIES

TO DO

NOTES:

Thursday

June 4th, 2020

6 am	
7	
8	
9	
10	
11	
12 pm	
1	
2	
3	
4	
5	
6	
7	
8	

PRIORITIES

TO DO

NOTES:

Friday

June 5th, 2020

6 am	
7	
8	
9	
10	
11	
12 pm	
1	
2	
3	
4	
5	
6	
7	
8	

PRIORITIES

TO DO

NOTES:

Saturday

June 6th, 2020

6 am	
7	
8	
9	
10	
11	
12 pm	
1	
2	
3	
4	
5	
6	
7	
8	

PRIORITIES

TO DO

NOTES:

Sunday

June 7th, 2020

6 am	
7	
8	
9	
10	
11	
12 pm	
1	
2	
3	
4	
5	
6	
7	
8	

PRIORITIES

TO DO

NOTES:

Monday

June 8th, 2020

6 am	
7	
8	
9	
10	
11	
12 pm	
1	
2	
3	
4	
5	
6	
7	
8	

PRIORITIES

TO DO

NOTES:

Tuesday

June 9th, 2020

6 am	
7	
8	
9	
10	
11	
12 pm	
1	
2	
3	
4	
5	
6	
7	
8	

PRIORITIES

TO DO

NOTES:

Wednesday

June 10th, 2020

6 am	
7	
8	
9	
10	
11	
12 pm	
1	
2	
3	
4	
5	
6	
7	
8	

PRIORITIES

TO DO

NOTES:

Thursday

June 11th, 2020

6 am	
7	
8	
9	
10	
11	
12 pm	
1	
2	
3	
4	
5	
6	
7	
8	

PRIORITIES

TO DO

NOTES:

Friday

June 12th, 2020

6 am	
7	
8	
9	
10	
11	
12 pm	
1	
2	
3	
4	
5	
6	
7	
8	

PRIORITIES

TO DO

NOTES:

Saturday

June 13th, 2020

6 am	
7	
8	
9	
10	
11	
12 pm	
1	
2	
3	
4	
5	
6	
7	
8	

PRIORITIES

TO DO

NOTES:

Cranberry Cookies

- **Ingredients:**
- 2 eggs
- 1.5 cups almond flour
- 1 Tablespoon coconut oil
- 3-4 Tablespoons coconut flour
- 1/2 cup dried cranberries

Instructions:

Preheat oven to 325 degrees.

Beat the eggs and set aside.

Combine almond flour, coconut oil, and dried cranberries in a bowl.

Add in the eggs and knead the ingredients with your hands. Dough will be wet and sticky.

Add in the coconut flour one tablespoon at a time to achieve a consistency that is easy to roll out and not overly sticky. This should take approximately 3-4 TBSP.

Roll out the dough and cut out the treats using heart shaped cookie cutters.
Place the treats on a cookie sheet lined with parchment paper.

Bake for 15-18 minutes or until crisp.

Sunday

June 14th, 2020

6 am	
7	
8	
9	
10	
11	
12 pm	
1	
2	
3	
4	
5	
6	
7	
8	

PRIORITIES

TO DO

NOTES:

Monday

June 15th, 2020

6 am	
7	
8	
9	
10	
11	
12 pm	
1	
2	
3	
4	
5	
6	
7	
8	

PRIORITIES

TO DO

NOTES:

Tuesday

June 16th, 2020

6 am	
7	
8	
9	
10	
11	
12 pm	
1	
2	
3	
4	
5	
6	
7	
8	

PRIORITIES

TO DO

NOTES:

Wednesday

June 17th, 2020

6 am	
7	
8	
9	
10	
11	
12 pm	
1	
2	
3	
4	
5	
6	
7	
8	

PRIORITIES

TO DO

NOTES:

Thursday

June 18th, 2020

6 am	
7	
8	
9	
10	
11	
12 pm	
1	
2	
3	
4	
5	
6	
7	
8	

PRIORITIES

TO DO

NOTES:

Friday

June 19th, 2020

6 am	
7	
8	
9	
10	
11	
12 pm	
1	
2	
3	
4	
5	
6	
7	
8	

PRIORITIES

TO DO

NOTES:

Saturday

June 20th, 2020

6 am	
7	
8	
9	
10	
11	
12 pm	
1	
2	
3	
4	
5	
6	
7	
8	

PRIORITIES

TO DO

NOTES:

Sunday

June 21st, 2020

6 am	
7	
8	
9	
10	
11	
12 pm	
1	
2	
3	
4	
5	
6	
7	
8	

PRIORITIES

TO DO

NOTES:

Monday

June 22nd, 2020

6 am	
7	
8	
9	
10	
11	
12 pm	
1	
2	
3	
4	
5	
6	
7	
8	

PRIORITIES

TO DO

NOTES:

Tuesday

June 23rd, 2020

6 am	
7	
8	
9	
10	
11	
12 pm	
1	
2	
3	
4	
5	
6	
7	
8	

PRIORITIES

TO DO

NOTES:

Wednesday

June 24th, 2020

6 am	
7	
8	
9	
10	
11	
12 pm	
1	
2	
3	
4	
5	
6	
7	
8	

PRIORITIES

TO DO

NOTES:

Thursday

June 25th, 2020

6 am	
7	
8	
9	
10	
11	
12 pm	
1	
2	
3	
4	
5	
6	
7	
8	

PRIORITIES

TO DO

NOTES:

Friday

June 26th, 2020

6 am	
7	
8	
9	
10	
11	
12 pm	
1	
2	
3	
4	
5	
6	
7	
8	

PRIORITIES

TO DO

NOTES:

Saturday

June 27th, 2020

6 am	
7	
8	
9	
10	
11	
12 pm	
1	
2	
3	
4	
5	
6	
7	
8	

NOTES:

PRIORITIES

TO DO

Sunday

June 28th, 2020

6 am	
7	
8	
9	
10	
11	
12 pm	
1	
2	
3	
4	
5	
6	
7	
8	

PRIORITIES

TO DO

NOTES:

Monday

June 29th, 2020

6 am	
7	
8	
9	
10	
11	
12 pm	
1	
2	
3	
4	
5	
6	
7	
8	

PRIORITIES

TO DO

NOTES:

Tuesday

June 30th, 2020

6 am	
7	
8	
9	
10	
11	
12 pm	
1	
2	
3	
4	
5	
6	
7	
8	

PRIORITIES

TO DO

NOTES:

Notes...

When my hooman is not around to distract me, that's when I think my deepest thoughts...

JULY

DOGS HAVE PERSONALITY. PERSONALITY GOES A LONG WAY

JULY 2020

Sun	Mon	Tue	Wed	Thu	Fri	Sat
28	29	30	1	2	3	4
5	6	7	8	9	10	11
12	13	14	15	16	17	18
19	20	21	22	23	24	25
26	27	28	29	30	31	1

Notes:

July Photo

Hardwood floors are not ideal for doin' the zoomies. No traction anywhere. This situation needs to be remedied, hooman.

EAR FLAPS STUCK IN THE COUCH!

Wednesday

July 1st, 2020

6 am	
7	
8	
9	
10	
11	
12 pm	
1	
2	
3	
4	
5	
6	
7	
8	

PRIORITIES

TO DO

NOTES:

Thursday

July 2nd, 2020

6 am	
7	
8	
9	
10	
11	
12 pm	
1	
2	
3	
4	
5	
6	
7	
8	

PRIORITIES

TO DO

NOTES:

Friday

July 3rd, 2020

6 am	
7	
8	
9	
10	
11	
12 pm	
1	
2	
3	
4	
5	
6	
7	
8	

PRIORITIES

TO DO

NOTES:

Saturday

July 4th, 2020

6 am	
7	
8	
9	
10	
11	
12 pm	
1	
2	
3	
4	
5	
6	
7	
8	

PRIORITIES

TO DO

NOTES:

Sunday

July 5th, 2020

6 am	
7	
8	
9	
10	
11	
12 pm	
1	
2	
3	
4	
5	
6	
7	
8	

PRIORITIES

TO DO

NOTES:

Monday

July 6th, 2020

6 am	
7	
8	
9	
10	
11	
12 pm	
1	
2	
3	
4	
5	
6	
7	
8	

PRIORITIES

TO DO

NOTES:

Tuesday

July 7th, 2020

6 am	
7	
8	
9	
10	
11	
12 pm	
1	
2	
3	
4	
5	
6	
7	
8	

PRIORITIES

TO DO

NOTES:

Wednesday

July 8th, 2020

6 am	
7	
8	
9	
10	
11	
12 pm	
1	
2	
3	
4	
5	
6	
7	
8	

PRIORITIES

TO DO

NOTES:

Thursday

July 9th, 2020

6 am	
7	
8	
9	
10	
11	
12 pm	
1	
2	
3	
4	
5	
6	
7	
8	

PRIORITIES

TO DO

NOTES:

Friday

July 10th, 2020

6 am	
7	
8	
9	
10	
11	
12 pm	
1	
2	
3	
4	
5	
6	
7	
8	

PRIORITIES

TO DO

NOTES:

Saturday

July 11th, 2020

6 am	
7	
8	
9	
10	
11	
12 pm	
1	
2	
3	
4	
5	
6	
7	
8	

PRIORITIES

TO DO

NOTES:

Sunday

July 12th, 2020

6 am	
7	
8	
9	
10	
11	
12 pm	
1	
2	
3	
4	
5	
6	
7	
8	

PRIORITIES

TO DO

NOTES:

Monday

July 13th, 2020

6 am	
7	
8	
9	
10	
11	
12 pm	
1	
2	
3	
4	
5	
6	
7	
8	

PRIORITIES

TO DO

NOTES:

Tuesday

July 14th, 2020

6 am	
7	
8	
9	
10	
11	
12 pm	
1	
2	
3	
4	
5	
6	
7	
8	

PRIORITIES

TO DO

NOTES:

Banana Peanut Butter Frozen Popsicles

Ingredients:

- 4 cups (32-ounce container) plain yogurt
- 1 large banana
- 4 tablespoons peanut butter
- Coconut or olive oil cooking spray
- Small treats for the popsicle sticks.

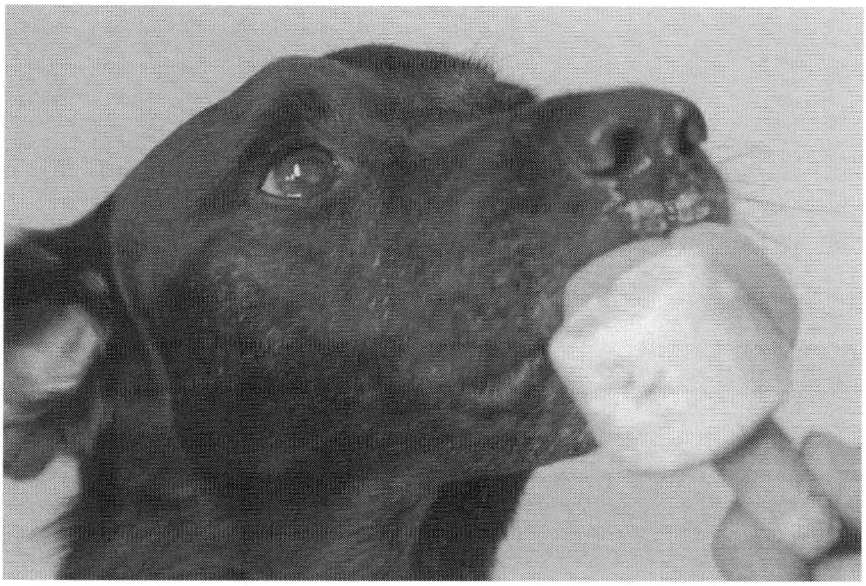

Instructions:

Blend yogurt, banana, and peanut butter in blender.

Place small cups in a rimmed baking pan and spray with cooking spray. (Instead of cups, you can use a silicone mold.)

Fill cups half way with yogurt mixture then place one treat in each cup to serve as an edible popsicle stick.

Transfer pan to freezer and freeze for 2 to 3 hours.

Remove a "pupsicle" from the freezer and hold onto the stick as your furry friend enjoys his treat. Once the frozen portion gets to be a manageable size, your dog can enjoy the treat on his own.

For dogs who are overeager and will want to chow these down right away, consider letting them soften a bit .

Wednesday

July 15th, 2020

6 am	
7	
8	
9	
10	
11	
12 pm	
1	
2	
3	
4	
5	
6	
7	
8	

PRIORITIES

TO DO

NOTES:

Thursday

July 16th, 2020

6 am	
7	
8	
9	
10	
11	
12 pm	
1	
2	
3	
4	
5	
6	
7	
8	

PRIORITIES

TO DO

NOTES:

Friday

July 17th, 2020

6 am	
7	
8	
9	
10	
11	
12 pm	
1	
2	
3	
4	
5	
6	
7	
8	

PRIORITIES

TO DO

NOTES:

Saturday

July 18th, 2020

6 am	
7	
8	
9	
10	
11	
12 pm	
1	
2	
3	
4	
5	
6	
7	
8	

PRIORITIES

TO DO

NOTES:

Sunday

July 19th, 2020

6 am	
7	
8	
9	
10	
11	
12 pm	
1	
2	
3	
4	
5	
6	
7	
8	

PRIORITIES

TO DO

NOTES:

Monday

July 20th, 2020

6 am	
7	
8	
9	
10	
11	
12 pm	
1	
2	
3	
4	
5	
6	
7	
8	

PRIORITIES

TO DO

NOTES:

Tuesday

July 21st, 2020

6 am	
7	
8	
9	
10	
11	
12 pm	
1	
2	
3	
4	
5	
6	
7	
8	

PRIORITIES

TO DO

NOTES:

Wednesday

July 22nd, 2020

6 am	
7	
8	
9	
10	
11	
12 pm	
1	
2	
3	
4	
5	
6	
7	
8	

PRIORITIES

TO DO

NOTES:

Thursday

July 23rd, 2020

6 am	
7	
8	
9	
10	
11	
12 pm	
1	
2	
3	
4	
5	
6	
7	
8	

PRIORITIES

TO DO

NOTES:

Friday

July 24th, 2020

6 am	
7	
8	
9	
10	
11	
12 pm	
1	
2	
3	
4	
5	
6	
7	
8	

PRIORITIES

TO DO

NOTES:

Saturday

July 25th, 2020

6 am	
7	
8	
9	
10	
11	
12 pm	
1	
2	
3	
4	
5	
6	
7	
8	

PRIORITIES

TO DO

NOTES:

Sunday

July 26th, 2020

6 am	
7	
8	
9	
10	
11	
12 pm	
1	
2	
3	
4	
5	
6	
7	
8	

PRIORITIES

TO DO

NOTES:

Monday

July 27th, 2020

6 am	
7	
8	
9	
10	
11	
12 pm	
1	
2	
3	
4	
5	
6	
7	
8	

PRIORITIES

TO DO

NOTES:

Tuesday

July 28th, 2020

6 am	
7	
8	
9	
10	
11	
12 pm	
1	
2	
3	
4	
5	
6	
7	
8	

PRIORITIES

TO DO

NOTES:

Wednesday

July 29th, 2020

6 am	
7	
8	
9	
10	
11	
12 pm	
1	
2	
3	
4	
5	
6	
7	
8	

PRIORITIES

TO DO

NOTES:

Thursday

July 30th, 2020

6 am	
7	
8	
9	
10	
11	
12 pm	
1	
2	
3	
4	
5	
6	
7	
8	

PRIORITIES

TO DO

NOTES:

Friday

July 31st, 2020

6 am	
7	
8	
9	
10	
11	
12 pm	
1	
2	
3	
4	
5	
6	
7	
8	

PRIORITIES

TO DO

NOTES:

Notes...

I AM THE BEST GUARD DOG. YOU CAN'T GET BY ME UNLESS YOU PET ME AND CALL ME A GOOD BOI...

THEN YOU CAN PASS BY QUITE EASILY.

AUGUST
I CALL MY DOG EGYPT BECAUSE HE LEAVES A PYRAMID IN EACH ROOM

AUGUST 2020

Sun	Mon	Tue	Wed	Thu	Fri	Sat
26	27	28	29	30	31	1
2	3	4	5	6	7	8
9	10	11	12	13	14	15
16	17	18	19	20	21	22
23	24	25	26	27	28	29
30	31	1	2	3	4	5

Notes:

August Photo

Bruce, the lizard, is staring at me through the screen door. "Bring it on, young doggo."

DOIN' ME A FRIGHTEN!

Saturday

August 1st, 2020

6 am	
7	
8	
9	
10	
11	
12 pm	
1	
2	
3	
4	
5	
6	
7	
8	

PRIORITIES

TO DO

NOTES:

Sunday

August 2nd, 2020

6 am	
7	
8	
9	
10	
11	
12 pm	
1	
2	
3	
4	
5	
6	
7	
8	

PRIORITIES

TO DO

NOTES:

Monday

August 3rd, 2020

6 am	
7	
8	
9	
10	
11	
12 pm	
1	
2	
3	
4	
5	
6	
7	
8	

PRIORITIES

TO DO

NOTES:

Tuesday

August 4th, 2020

6 am	
7	
8	
9	
10	
11	
12 pm	
1	
2	
3	
4	
5	
6	
7	
8	

PRIORITIES

TO DO

NOTES:

Wednesday

August 5th, 2020

6 am	
7	
8	
9	
10	
11	
12 pm	
1	
2	
3	
4	
5	
6	
7	
8	

PRIORITIES

TO DO

NOTES:

Thursday

August 6th, 2020

6 am	
7	
8	
9	
10	
11	
12 pm	
1	
2	
3	
4	
5	
6	
7	
8	

PRIORITIES

TO DO

NOTES:

Friday

August 7th, 2020

6 am	
7	
8	
9	
10	
11	
12 pm	
1	
2	
3	
4	
5	
6	
7	
8	

PRIORITIES

TO DO

NOTES:

Saturday

August 8th, 2020

6 am	
7	
8	
9	
10	
11	
12 pm	
1	
2	
3	
4	
5	
6	
7	
8	

PRIORITIES

TO DO

NOTES:

Sunday

August 9th, 2020

6 am	
7	
8	
9	
10	
11	
12 pm	
1	
2	
3	
4	
5	
6	
7	
8	

PRIORITIES

TO DO

NOTES:

Monday

August 10th, 2020

6 am	
7	
8	
9	
10	
11	
12 pm	
1	
2	
3	
4	
5	
6	
7	
8	

PRIORITIES

TO DO

NOTES:

Tuesday

August 11th, 2020

6 am	
7	
8	
9	
10	
11	
12 pm	
1	
2	
3	
4	
5	
6	
7	
8	

PRIORITIES

TO DO

NOTES:

Wednesday

August 12th, 2020

6 am	
7	
8	
9	
10	
11	
12 pm	
1	
2	
3	
4	
5	
6	
7	
8	

PRIORITIES

TO DO

NOTES:

Thursday

August 13th, 2020

6 am	
7	
8	
9	
10	
11	
12 pm	
1	
2	
3	
4	
5	
6	
7	
8	

PRIORITIES

TO DO

NOTES:

Friday

August 14th, 2020

6 am	
7	
8	
9	
10	
11	
12 pm	
1	
2	
3	
4	
5	
6	
7	
8	

PRIORITIES

TO DO

NOTES:

Pumpkin Apple Dog Treats

Ingredients:

- 4 - 4.5 cups oatmeal, plus additional
- 1 medium apple
- 1 egg
- 1 CUP canned pumpkin

Instructions:

Preheat oven to 400 degrees F.

Grind the oatmeal down in a food processor or blender. Transfer to mixing bowl.

Core apple, being sure to remove all of the seeds. Grate apple, and add to bowl with oatmeal.

Add egg and canned pumpkin to bowl and mix well to combine. The mixture will be thick and slightly sticky.

On a surface dusted with oatmeal (ground or not, your choice) roll the dough out to approximately 1/2" thick. Use a doggy bone cookie cutter to cut dough into shapes, and transfer to a lined baking sheet.

Bake for approximately 12-15 minutes, or until golden and crispy. Allow to cool to room temperature, then store in an airtight container for up to a week.

Saturday

August 15th, 2020

6 am	
7	
8	
9	
10	
11	
12 pm	
1	
2	
3	
4	
5	
6	
7	
8	

PRIORITIES

TO DO

NOTES:

Sunday

August 16th, 2020

6 am	
7	
8	
9	
10	
11	
12 pm	
1	
2	
3	
4	
5	
6	
7	
8	

PRIORITIES

TO DO

NOTES:

Monday

August 17th, 2020

6 am	
7	
8	
9	
10	
11	
12 pm	
1	
2	
3	
4	
5	
6	
7	
8	

PRIORITIES

TO DO

NOTES:

Tuesday

August 18th, 2020

6 am	
7	
8	
9	
10	
11	
12 pm	
1	
2	
3	
4	
5	
6	
7	
8	

PRIORITIES

TO DO

NOTES:

Wednesday

August 19th, 2020

6 am	
7	
8	
9	
10	
11	
12 pm	
1	
2	
3	
4	
5	
6	
7	
8	

PRIORITIES

TO DO

NOTES:

Thursday

August 20th, 2020

6 am	
7	
8	
9	
10	
11	
12 pm	
1	
2	
3	
4	
5	
6	
7	
8	

PRIORITIES

TO DO

NOTES:

Friday

August 21st, 2020

6 am	
7	
8	
9	
10	
11	
12 pm	
1	
2	
3	
4	
5	
6	
7	
8	

PRIORITIES

TO DO

NOTES:

Saturday

August 22nd, 2020

6 am	
7	
8	
9	
10	
11	
12 pm	
1	
2	
3	
4	
5	
6	
7	
8	

PRIORITIES

TO DO

NOTES:

Sunday

August 23rd, 2020

6 am	
7	
8	
9	
10	
11	
12 pm	
1	
2	
3	
4	
5	
6	
7	
8	

PRIORITIES

TO DO

NOTES:

Monday

August 24th, 2020

6 am	
7	
8	
9	
10	
11	
12 pm	
1	
2	
3	
4	
5	
6	
7	
8	

PRIORITIES

TO DO

NOTES:

Tuesday

August 25th, 2020

6 am	
7	
8	
9	
10	
11	
12 pm	
1	
2	
3	
4	
5	
6	
7	
8	

PRIORITIES

TO DO

NOTES:

Wednesday

August 26th, 2020

6 am	
7	
8	
9	
10	
11	
12 pm	
1	
2	
3	
4	
5	
6	
7	
8	

PRIORITIES

TO DO

NOTES:

Thursday

August 27th, 2020

6 am	
7	
8	
9	
10	
11	
12 pm	
1	
2	
3	
4	
5	
6	
7	
8	

PRIORITIES

TO DO

NOTES:

Friday

August 28th, 2020

6 am	
7	
8	
9	
10	
11	
12 pm	
1	
2	
3	
4	
5	
6	
7	
8	

PRIORITIES

TO DO

NOTES:

Saturday

August 29th, 2020

6 am	
7	
8	
9	
10	
11	
12 pm	
1	
2	
3	
4	
5	
6	
7	
8	

PRIORITIES

TO DO

NOTES:

Sunday

August 30th, 2020

6 am	
7	
8	
9	
10	
11	
12 pm	
1	
2	
3	
4	
5	
6	
7	
8	

PRIORITIES

TO DO

NOTES:

Monday

August 31st, 2020

6 am	
7	
8	
9	
10	
11	
12 pm	
1	
2	
3	
4	
5	
6	
7	
8	

PRIORITIES

TO DO

NOTES:

Notes...

My fren and me love:

...good tail wags

...cheese & chimkin

...invading your space

chasing Bruce -the lizard

peanut butter (oh yes!!)

Speedy zoomies

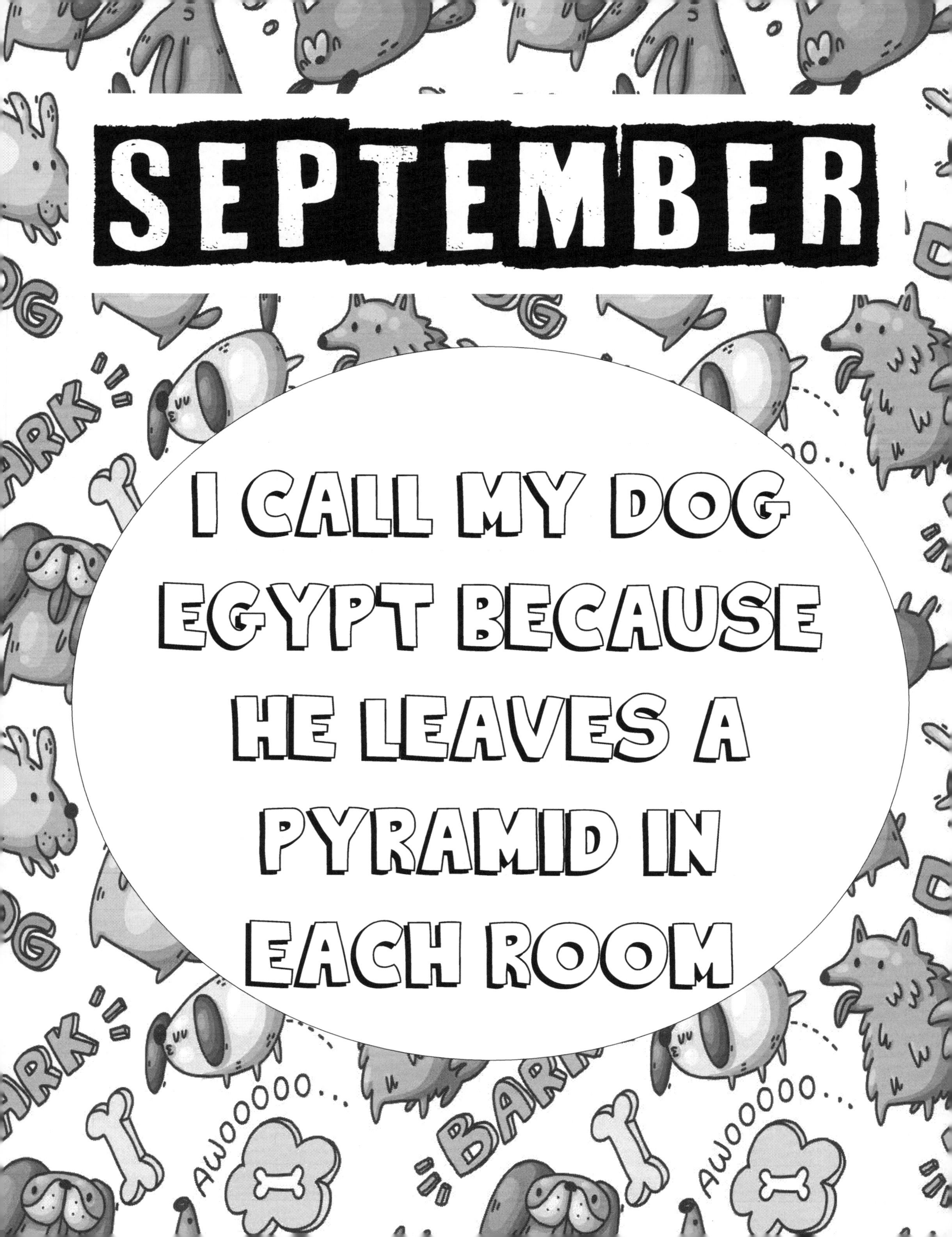

SEPTEMBER

I CALL MY DOG EGYPT BECAUSE HE LEAVES A PYRAMID IN EACH ROOM

SEPTEMBER 2020

Sun	Mon	Tue	Wed	Thu	Fri	Sat
30	31	1	2	3	4	5
6	7	8	9	10	11	12
13	14	15	16	17	18	19
20	21	22	23	24	25	26
27	28	29	30	1	2	3

Notes:

September Photo

If I am ignored, I will notify the hooman via a series of discreet borfs. The offender will then be removed from the house.

IMMEDIATELY!

Tuesday

September 1st, 2020

6 am	
7	
8	
9	
10	
11	
12 pm	
1	
2	
3	
4	
5	
6	
7	
8	

PRIORITIES

TO DO

NOTES:

Wednesday

September 2nd, 2020

6 am	
7	
8	
9	
10	
11	
12 pm	
1	
2	
3	
4	
5	
6	
7	
8	

PRIORITIES

TO DO

NOTES:

Thursday

September 3rd, 2020

6 am	
7	
8	
9	
10	
11	
12 pm	
1	
2	
3	
4	
5	
6	
7	
8	

PRIORITIES

TO DO

NOTES:

Friday

September 4th, 2020

6 am	
7	
8	
9	
10	
11	
12 pm	
1	
2	
3	
4	
5	
6	
7	
8	

PRIORITIES

TO DO

NOTES:

Saturday

September 5th, 2020

6 am	
7	
8	
9	
10	
11	
12 pm	
1	
2	
3	
4	
5	
6	
7	
8	

PRIORITIES

TO DO

NOTES:

Sunday

September 6th, 2020

6 am	
7	
8	
9	
10	
11	
12 pm	
1	
2	
3	
4	
5	
6	
7	
8	

PRIORITIES

TO DO

NOTES:

Monday

September 7th, 2020

6 am	
7	
8	
9	
10	
11	
12 pm	
1	
2	
3	
4	
5	
6	
7	
8	

PRIORITIES

TO DO

NOTES:

Tuesday

September 8th, 2020

6 am	
7	
8	
9	
10	
11	
12 pm	
1	
2	
3	
4	
5	
6	
7	
8	

PRIORITIES

TO DO

NOTES:

Wednesday

September 9th, 2020

6 am	
7	
8	
9	
10	
11	
12 pm	
1	
2	
3	
4	
5	
6	
7	
8	

PRIORITIES

TO DO

NOTES:

Thursday

September 10th, 2020

6 am	
7	
8	
9	
10	
11	
12 pm	
1	
2	
3	
4	
5	
6	
7	
8	

PRIORITIES

TO DO

NOTES:

Friday

September 11th, 2020

6 am	
7	
8	
9	
10	
11	
12 pm	
1	
2	
3	
4	
5	
6	
7	
8	

PRIORITIES

TO DO

NOTES:

Saturday

September 12th, 2020

6 am	
7	
8	
9	
10	
11	
12 pm	
1	
2	
3	
4	
5	
6	
7	
8	

PRIORITIES

TO DO

NOTES:

Sunday

September 13th, 2020

6 am	
7	
8	
9	
10	
11	
12 pm	
1	
2	
3	
4	
5	
6	
7	
8	

PRIORITIES

TO DO

NOTES:

Monday

September 14th, 2020

6 am	
7	
8	
9	
10	
11	
12 pm	
1	
2	
3	
4	
5	
6	
7	
8	

PRIORITIES

TO DO

NOTES:

Sweet Potato Fries Treats

Ingredients:

- 1 Sweet Potato
- 1 tbsp Coconut Oil (melted)
- Spices - Turmeric, Cinnamon

Instructions:

Preheat oven to 425 degrees F.

Wash and peel the sweet potato.

Cut the sweet potato into evenly sized long skinny (fry shaped) pieces.

Coat with oil and spices - Mix in a large bowl or Ziploc bag.

Place fries on baking sheet in one layer.

Bake for 15 minutes.

Flip over fries for even baking.

Bake for another 10-15 minutes.

Let cool before giving to your dog!

Dog Safe Spices
Basil. Cinnamon
Coriander, Dill
Ginger, Marjoram
Oregano, Parsley,
Rosemary, Sage
Tarragon, Thyme
Turmeric

Tuesday

September 15th, 2020

6 am	
7	
8	
9	
10	
11	
12 pm	
1	
2	
3	
4	
5	
6	
7	
8	

PRIORITIES

TO DO

NOTES:

Wednesday

September 16th, 2020

6 am	
7	
8	
9	
10	
11	
12 pm	
1	
2	
3	
4	
5	
6	
7	
8	

PRIORITIES

TO DO

NOTES:

Thursday

September 17th, 2020

6 am	
7	
8	
9	
10	
11	
12 pm	
1	
2	
3	
4	
5	
6	
7	
8	

PRIORITIES

TO DO

NOTES:

Friday

September 18th, 2020

6 am	
7	
8	
9	
10	
11	
12 pm	
1	
2	
3	
4	
5	
6	
7	
8	

PRIORITIES

TO DO

NOTES:

Saturday

September 19th, 2020

6 am	
7	
8	
9	
10	
11	
12 pm	
1	
2	
3	
4	
5	
6	
7	
8	

PRIORITIES

TO DO

NOTES:

Sunday

September 20th, 2020

6 am	
7	
8	
9	
10	
11	
12 pm	
1	
2	
3	
4	
5	
6	
7	
8	

PRIORITIES

TO DO

NOTES:

Monday

September 21st, 2020

6 am	
7	
8	
9	
10	
11	
12 pm	
1	
2	
3	
4	
5	
6	
7	
8	

PRIORITIES

TO DO

NOTES:

Tuesday

September 22nd, 2020

6 am	
7	
8	
9	
10	
11	
12 pm	
1	
2	
3	
4	
5	
6	
7	
8	

PRIORITIES

TO DO

NOTES:

Wednesday

September 23rd, 2020

6 am	
7	
8	
9	
10	
11	
12 pm	
1	
2	
3	
4	
5	
6	
7	
8	

PRIORITIES

TO DO

NOTES:

Thursday

September 24th, 2020

6 am	
7	
8	
9	
10	
11	
12 pm	
1	
2	
3	
4	
5	
6	
7	
8	

PRIORITIES

TO DO

NOTES:

Friday

September 25th, 2020

6 am	
7	
8	
9	
10	
11	
12 pm	
1	
2	
3	
4	
5	
6	
7	
8	

PRIORITIES

TO DO

NOTES:

Saturday

September 26th, 2020

6 am	
7	
8	
9	
10	
11	
12 pm	
1	
2	
3	
4	
5	
6	
7	
8	

PRIORITIES

TO DO

NOTES:

Sunday

September 27th, 2020

6 am	
7	
8	
9	
10	
11	
12 pm	
1	
2	
3	
4	
5	
6	
7	
8	

PRIORITIES

TO DO

NOTES:

Monday

September 28th, 2020

6 am	
7	
8	
9	
10	
11	
12 pm	
1	
2	
3	
4	
5	
6	
7	
8	

PRIORITIES

TO DO

NOTES:

Tuesday

September 29th, 2020

6 am	
7	
8	
9	
10	
11	
12 pm	
1	
2	
3	
4	
5	
6	
7	
8	

PRIORITIES

TO DO

NOTES:

Wednesday

September 30th, 2020

6 am	
7	
8	
9	
10	
11	
12 pm	
1	
2	
3	
4	
5	
6	
7	
8	

PRIORITIES

TO DO

NOTES:

Notes...

These are my frens...we are all
good bois.
...we love zoomies
...we bork
But only to protect you
..we love, we listen
...we love some more.
Is there any chimkin?

OCTOBER

DOGS DO SPEAK BUT ONLY TO THOSE WHO KNOW HOW TO LISTEN

OCTOBER 2020

Sun	Mon	Tue	Wed	Thu	Fri	Sat
27	28	29	30	1	2	3
4	5	6	7	8	9	10
11	12	13	14	15	16	17
18	19	20	21	22	23	24
25	26	27	28	29	30	31

Notes:

October Photo

Some say a dog's life is easy...no worries, no taxes. I say, walk a mile in my shoes. That reminds me, I took your shoe.

SORRY, HOOMAN!

Thursday

October 1st, 2020

6 am	
7	
8	
9	
10	
11	
12 pm	
1	
2	
3	
4	
5	
6	
7	
8	

PRIORITIES

TO DO

NOTES:

Friday

October 2nd, 2020

6 am	
7	
8	
9	
10	
11	
12 pm	
1	
2	
3	
4	
5	
6	
7	
8	

PRIORITIES

TO DO

NOTES:

Saturday

October 3rd, 2020

6 am	
7	
8	
9	
10	
11	
12 pm	
1	
2	
3	
4	
5	
6	
7	
8	

PRIORITIES

TO DO

NOTES:

Sunday

October 4th, 2020

6 am	
7	
8	
9	
10	
11	
12 pm	
1	
2	
3	
4	
5	
6	
7	
8	

PRIORITIES

TO DO

NOTES:

Monday

October 5th, 2020

6 am	
7	
8	
9	
10	
11	
12 pm	
1	
2	
3	
4	
5	
6	
7	
8	

PRIORITIES

TO DO

NOTES:

Tuesday

October 6th, 2020

6 am	
7	
8	
9	
10	
11	
12 pm	
1	
2	
3	
4	
5	
6	
7	
8	

PRIORITIES

TO DO

NOTES:

Wednesday

October 7th, 2020

6 am	
7	
8	
9	
10	
11	
12 pm	
1	
2	
3	
4	
5	
6	
7	
8	

PRIORITIES

TO DO

NOTES:

Thursday

October 8th, 2020

6 am	
7	
8	
9	
10	
11	
12 pm	
1	
2	
3	
4	
5	
6	
7	
8	

PRIORITIES

TO DO

NOTES:

Friday

October 9th, 2020

6 am	
7	
8	
9	
10	
11	
12 pm	
1	
2	
3	
4	
5	
6	
7	
8	

PRIORITIES

TO DO

NOTES:

Saturday

October 10th, 2020

6 am	
7	
8	
9	
10	
11	
12 pm	
1	
2	
3	
4	
5	
6	
7	
8	

PRIORITIES

TO DO

NOTES:

Sunday

October 11th, 2020

6 am	
7	
8	
9	
10	
11	
12 pm	
1	
2	
3	
4	
5	
6	
7	
8	

PRIORITIES

TO DO

NOTES:

Monday

October 12th, 2020

6 am	
7	
8	
9	
10	
11	
12 pm	
1	
2	
3	
4	
5	
6	
7	
8	

PRIORITIES

TO DO

NOTES:

Tuesday

October 13th, 2020

6 am	
7	
8	
9	
10	
11	
12 pm	
1	
2	
3	
4	
5	
6	
7	
8	

PRIORITIES

TO DO

NOTES:

Wednesday

October 14th, 2020

6 am	
7	
8	
9	
10	
11	
12 pm	
1	
2	
3	
4	
5	
6	
7	
8	

PRIORITIES

TO DO

NOTES:

Thursday

October 15th, 2020

6 am	
7	
8	
9	
10	
11	
12 pm	
1	
2	
3	
4	
5	
6	
7	
8	

PRIORITIES

TO DO

NOTES:

Friday

October 16th, 2020

6 am	
7	
8	
9	
10	
11	
12 pm	
1	
2	
3	
4	
5	
6	
7	
8	

PRIORITIES

TO DO

NOTES:

Saturday

October 17th, 2020

6 am	
7	
8	
9	
10	
11	
12 pm	
1	
2	
3	
4	
5	
6	
7	
8	

PRIORITIES

TO DO

NOTES:

Sunday

October 18th, 2020

6 am	
7	
8	
9	
10	
11	
12 pm	
1	
2	
3	
4	
5	
6	
7	
8	

PRIORITIES

TO DO

NOTES:

Monday

October 19th, 2020

6 am	
7	
8	
9	
10	
11	
12 pm	
1	
2	
3	
4	
5	
6	
7	
8	

PRIORITIES

TO DO

NOTES:

Tuesday

October 20th, 2020

6 am	
7	
8	
9	
10	
11	
12 pm	
1	
2	
3	
4	
5	
6	
7	
8	

PRIORITIES

TO DO

NOTES:

Spoiled Dog Birthday Cake

NATIONAL SPOIL YOUR DOG DAY
Monday, August 20, 2020

Ingredients:

Cake
- 1 cup flour
- 1/2 tsp baking soda
- 1/8 cup vegetable oil
- 1/4 cup peanut butter
- 1/2 cup applesauce
- 1/2 cup pumpkin puree
- 1 egg

Frosting
- 1/2 cup plain Greek yogurt
- 1/4 cup peanut butter

Instructions:

Cake

Preheat oven to 350 degrees F.

In a large bowl, combine flour and baking soda.

In a separate bowl mix together vegetable oil, peanut butter, applesauce and pumpkin puree. Once combined, mix in egg and mix until combined.

Combine wet and dry ingredients and stir until combined.

Pour mixture into an 8" round pan (a square pan can also be used) that has been greased with oil.

Bake for approximately 25-30 minutes or until a toothpick inserted into the center comes out clean and the cake springs back when pressed lightly.

Cake
Allow to cool on a wire rack prior to removing from pan.

After cooling, add frosting if desired.

Frosting
Mix Greek yogurt and peanut butter until well combined. Spread over cake. If not serving immediately, store in refrigerator.

Wednesday

October 21st, 2020

6 am	
7	
8	
9	
10	
11	
12 pm	
1	
2	
3	
4	
5	
6	
7	
8	

PRIORITIES

TO DO

NOTES:

Thursday

October 22nd, 2020

6 am	
7	
8	
9	
10	
11	
12 pm	
1	
2	
3	
4	
5	
6	
7	
8	

PRIORITIES

TO DO

NOTES:

Friday

October 23rd, 2020

6 am	
7	
8	
9	
10	
11	
12 pm	
1	
2	
3	
4	
5	
6	
7	
8	

PRIORITIES

TO DO

NOTES:

Saturday

October 24th, 2020

6 am	
7	
8	
9	
10	
11	
12 pm	
1	
2	
3	
4	
5	
6	
7	
8	

PRIORITIES

TO DO

NOTES:

Sunday

October 25th, 2020

6 am	
7	
8	
9	
10	
11	
12 pm	
1	
2	
3	
4	
5	
6	
7	
8	

PRIORITIES

TO DO

NOTES:

Monday

October 26th, 2020

6 am	
7	
8	
9	
10	
11	
12 pm	
1	
2	
3	
4	
5	
6	
7	
8	

PRIORITIES

TO DO

NOTES:

Tuesday

October 27th, 2020

6 am	
7	
8	
9	
10	
11	
12 pm	
1	
2	
3	
4	
5	
6	
7	
8	

PRIORITIES

TO DO

NOTES:

Wednesday

October 28th, 2020

6 am	
7	
8	
9	
10	
11	
12 pm	
1	
2	
3	
4	
5	
6	
7	
8	

PRIORITIES

TO DO

NOTES:

Thursday

October 29th, 2020

6 am	
7	
8	
9	
10	
11	
12 pm	
1	
2	
3	
4	
5	
6	
7	
8	

PRIORITIES

TO DO

NOTES:

Friday

October 30th, 2020

6 am	
7	
8	
9	
10	
11	
12 pm	
1	
2	
3	
4	
5	
6	
7	
8	

PRIORITIES

TO DO

NOTES:

Saturday

October 31st, 2020

6 am	
7	
8	
9	
10	
11	
12 pm	
1	
2	
3	
4	
5	
6	
7	
8	

PRIORITIES

TO DO

NOTES:

Notes...

MY FREN AND ME ARE GETTING ALONG REAL WELL. WE ALTERNATE BORKS, WOOFS AND GRRBORKS

FOR ULTIMATE PROTECT.

NOVEMBER

THE ROAD TO MY HEART IS PAVED WITH PAW PRINTS

NOVEMBER 2020

Sun	Mon	Tue	Wed	Thu	Fri	Sat
1	2	3	4	5	6	7
8	9	10	11	12	13	14
15	16	17	18	19	20	21
22	23	24	25	26	27	28
29	30	1	2	3	4	5

Notes:

November Photo

My most fancy tricks...
Snoozing, sit (a classic), the fetch, trot/advanced walk, roll, zoom (speedy), begging for chimkin.

SORTED BY DIFFICULTY!

Sunday

November 1st, 2020

6 am	
7	
8	
9	
10	
11	
12 pm	
1	
2	
3	
4	
5	
6	
7	
8	

PRIORITIES

TO DO

NOTES:

Monday

November 2nd, 2020

6 am	
7	
8	
9	
10	
11	
12 pm	
1	
2	
3	
4	
5	
6	
7	
8	

PRIORITIES

TO DO

NOTES:

Tuesday

November 3rd, 2020

6 am	
7	
8	
9	
10	
11	
12 pm	
1	
2	
3	
4	
5	
6	
7	
8	

PRIORITIES

TO DO

NOTES:

Wednesday

November 4th, 2020

6 am	
7	
8	
9	
10	
11	
12 pm	
1	
2	
3	
4	
5	
6	
7	
8	

PRIORITIES

TO DO

NOTES:

Thursday

November 5th, 2020

6 am	
7	
8	
9	
10	
11	
12 pm	
1	
2	
3	
4	
5	
6	
7	
8	

PRIORITIES

TO DO

NOTES:

Friday

November 6th, 2020

6 am	
7	
8	
9	
10	
11	
12 pm	
1	
2	
3	
4	
5	
6	
7	
8	

PRIORITIES

TO DO

NOTES:

Saturday

November 7th, 2020

6 am	
7	
8	
9	
10	
11	
12 pm	
1	
2	
3	
4	
5	
6	
7	
8	

PRIORITIES

TO DO

NOTES:

Sunday

November 8th, 2020

6 am	
7	
8	
9	
10	
11	
12 pm	
1	
2	
3	
4	
5	
6	
7	
8	

PRIORITIES

TO DO

NOTES:

Monday

November 9th, 2020

6 am	
7	
8	
9	
10	
11	
12 pm	
1	
2	
3	
4	
5	
6	
7	
8	

PRIORITIES

TO DO

NOTES:

Tuesday

November 10th, 2020

6 am	
7	
8	
9	
10	
11	
12 pm	
1	
2	
3	
4	
5	
6	
7	
8	

PRIORITIES

TO DO

NOTES:

Wednesday

November 11th, 2020

6 am	
7	
8	
9	
10	
11	
12 pm	
1	
2	
3	
4	
5	
6	
7	
8	

PRIORITIES

TO DO

NOTES:

Thursday

November 12th, 2020

6 am	
7	
8	
9	
10	
11	
12 pm	
1	
2	
3	
4	
5	
6	
7	
8	

PRIORITIES

TO DO

NOTES:

Friday

November 13th, 2020

6 am	
7	
8	
9	
10	
11	
12 pm	
1	
2	
3	
4	
5	
6	
7	
8	

PRIORITIES

TO DO

NOTES:

Saturday

November 14th, 2020

6 am	
7	
8	
9	
10	
11	
12 pm	
1	
2	
3	
4	
5	
6	
7	
8	

PRIORITIES

TO DO

NOTES:

Grain-Free Dog Treats

Ingredients:

- 2 cups coconut flour
- ½ teaspoon baking soda
- ½ teaspoon cinnamon
- 1 can 15 oz. pure pumpkin
- ½ cup peanut butter
- ½ cup coconut oil melted
- 4 eggs

Peanut Butter Drizzle:

- 1/3 cup peanut butter
- 1-2 tablespoons melted coconut oil

Instructions:

Preheat oven to 350 degrees F.

Add eggs to large bowl and beat. Add the remaining ingredients and stir together until a soft dough forms.

Place on parchment paper and carefully roll dough out with a rolling pin (you may need to put another piece of parchment paper on top so it doesn't stick to rolling pin).

Cut dough into shapes with cookie cutters and gently transfer to baking sheet lined with parchment paper.

Bake for 12 to 18 minutes, or until treats are hard. Remove from oven and cool for 5 minutes on baking sheet. Transfer to cooling rack.

For peanut butter drizzle, combine melted coconut oil and peanut butter and drizzle over treats.

Store in airtight container at room temperature or in the refrigerator up to one week. Store in the freezer for a month.

Sunday

November 15th, 2020

6 am	
7	
8	
9	
10	
11	
12 pm	
1	
2	
3	
4	
5	
6	
7	
8	

PRIORITIES

TO DO

NOTES:

Monday

November 16th, 2020

6 am	
7	
8	
9	
10	
11	
12 pm	
1	
2	
3	
4	
5	
6	
7	
8	

PRIORITIES

TO DO

NOTES:

Tuesday

November 17th, 2020

6 am	
7	
8	
9	
10	
11	
12 pm	
1	
2	
3	
4	
5	
6	
7	
8	

PRIORITIES

TO DO

NOTES:

Wednesday

November 18th, 2020

6 am	
7	
8	
9	
10	
11	
12 pm	
1	
2	
3	
4	
5	
6	
7	
8	

PRIORITIES

TO DO

NOTES:

Thursday

November 19th, 2020

6 am	
7	
8	
9	
10	
11	
12 pm	
1	
2	
3	
4	
5	
6	
7	
8	

PRIORITIES

TO DO

NOTES:

Friday

November 20th, 2020

6 am	
7	
8	
9	
10	
11	
12 pm	
1	
2	
3	
4	
5	
6	
7	
8	

PRIORITIES

TO DO

NOTES:

Saturday

November 21st, 2020

6 am	
7	
8	
9	
10	
11	
12 pm	
1	
2	
3	
4	
5	
6	
7	
8	

PRIORITIES

TO DO

NOTES:

Sunday

November 22nd, 2020

6 am	
7	
8	
9	
10	
11	
12 pm	
1	
2	
3	
4	
5	
6	
7	
8	

PRIORITIES

TO DO

NOTES:

Monday

November 23rd, 2020

6 am	
7	
8	
9	
10	
11	
12 pm	
1	
2	
3	
4	
5	
6	
7	
8	

PRIORITIES

TO DO

NOTES:

Tuesday

November 24th, 2020

6 am	
7	
8	
9	
10	
11	
12 pm	
1	
2	
3	
4	
5	
6	
7	
8	

PRIORITIES

TO DO

NOTES:

Wednesday

November 25th, 2020

6 am	
7	
8	
9	
10	
11	
12 pm	
1	
2	
3	
4	
5	
6	
7	
8	

PRIORITIES

TO DO

NOTES:

Thursday

November 26th, 2020

6 am	
7	
8	
9	
10	
11	
12 pm	
1	
2	
3	
4	
5	
6	
7	
8	

PRIORITIES

TO DO

NOTES:

Friday

November 27th, 2020

6 am	
7	
8	
9	
10	
11	
12 pm	
1	
2	
3	
4	
5	
6	
7	
8	

PRIORITIES

TO DO

NOTES:

Saturday

November 28th, 2020

6 am	
7	
8	
9	
10	
11	
12 pm	
1	
2	
3	
4	
5	
6	
7	
8	

PRIORITIES

TO DO

NOTES:

Sunday

November 29th, 2020

6 am	
7	
8	
9	
10	
11	
12 pm	
1	
2	
3	
4	
5	
6	
7	
8	

PRIORITIES

TO DO

NOTES:

Monday

November 30th, 2020

6 am	
7	
8	
9	
10	
11	
12 pm	
1	
2	
3	
4	
5	
6	
7	
8	

PRIORITIES

TO DO

NOTES:

Notes...

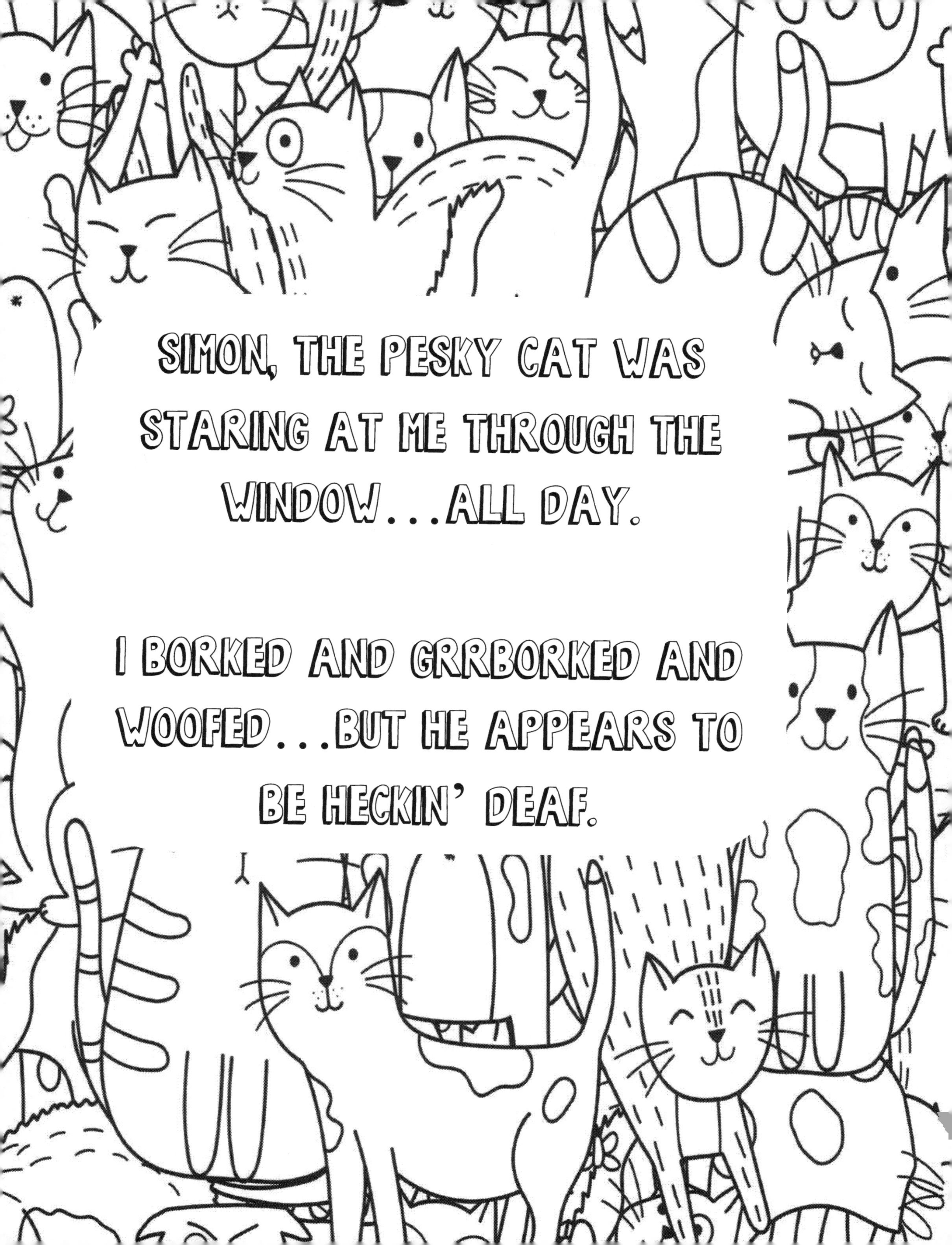

SIMON, THE PESKY CAT WAS STARING AT ME THROUGH THE WINDOW...ALL DAY.

I BORKED AND GRRBORKED AND WOOFED...BUT HE APPEARS TO BE HECKIN' DEAF.

DECEMBER

MY LITTLE DOG — A HEARTBEAT AT MY FEET

DECEMBER 2020

Sun	Mon	Tue	Wed	Thu	Fri	Sat
29	30	1	2	3	4	5
6	7	8	9	10	11	12
13	14	15	16	17	18	19
20	21	22	23	24	25	26
27	28	29	30	31	1	2

Notes:

December Photo

The hooman said we could go on a car ride tomorrow when he gets home. I'm so happy, I can't even snooze.

TAIL IS WAGGING SO FAST!

Tuesday

December 1st, 2020

6 am	
7	
8	
9	
10	
11	
12 pm	
1	
2	
3	
4	
5	
6	
7	
8	

PRIORITIES

TO DO

NOTES:

Wednesday

December 2nd, 2020

6 am	
7	
8	
9	
10	
11	
12 pm	
1	
2	
3	
4	
5	
6	
7	
8	

PRIORITIES

TO DO

NOTES:

Thursday

December 3rd, 2020

6 am	
7	
8	
9	
10	
11	
12 pm	
1	
2	
3	
4	
5	
6	
7	
8	

PRIORITIES

TO DO

NOTES:

Friday

December 4th, 2020

6 am	
7	
8	
9	
10	
11	
12 pm	
1	
2	
3	
4	
5	
6	
7	
8	

PRIORITIES

TO DO

NOTES:

Saturday

December 5th, 2020

6 am	
7	
8	
9	
10	
11	
12 pm	
1	
2	
3	
4	
5	
6	
7	
8	

PRIORITIES

TO DO

NOTES:

Sunday

December 6th, 2020

6 am	
7	
8	
9	
10	
11	
12 pm	
1	
2	
3	
4	
5	
6	
7	
8	

PRIORITIES

TO DO

NOTES:

Monday

December 7th, 2020

6 am	
7	
8	
9	
10	
11	
12 pm	
1	
2	
3	
4	
5	
6	
7	
8	

PRIORITIES

TO DO

NOTES:

Tuesday

December 8th, 2020

6 am	
7	
8	
9	
10	
11	
12 pm	
1	
2	
3	
4	
5	
6	
7	
8	

PRIORITIES

TO DO

NOTES:

Wednesday

December 9th, 2020

6 am	
7	
8	
9	
10	
11	
12 pm	
1	
2	
3	
4	
5	
6	
7	
8	

PRIORITIES

TO DO

NOTES:

Thursday

December 10th, 2020

6 am	
7	
8	
9	
10	
11	
12 pm	
1	
2	
3	
4	
5	
6	
7	
8	

PRIORITIES

TO DO

NOTES:

Friday

December 11th, 2020

6 am	
7	
8	
9	
10	
11	
12 pm	
1	
2	
3	
4	
5	
6	
7	
8	

PRIORITIES

TO DO

NOTES:

Saturday

December 12th, 2020

6 am	
7	
8	
9	
10	
11	
12 pm	
1	
2	
3	
4	
5	
6	
7	
8	

PRIORITIES

TO DO

NOTES:

Sunday

December 13th, 2020

6 am	
7	
8	
9	
10	
11	
12 pm	
1	
2	
3	
4	
5	
6	
7	
8	

PRIORITIES

TO DO

NOTES:

Monday

December 14th, 2020

6 am	
7	
8	
9	
10	
11	
12 pm	
1	
2	
3	
4	
5	
6	
7	
8	

PRIORITIES

TO DO

NOTES:

Peppermint Holi-Dog Treats

Ingredients:

- 3 cups whole wheat flour
- 1 cup water
- 1 tsp molasses
- 2 Tbs peanut butter
- 2 Tbs olive oil
- 1 tsp peppermint extract

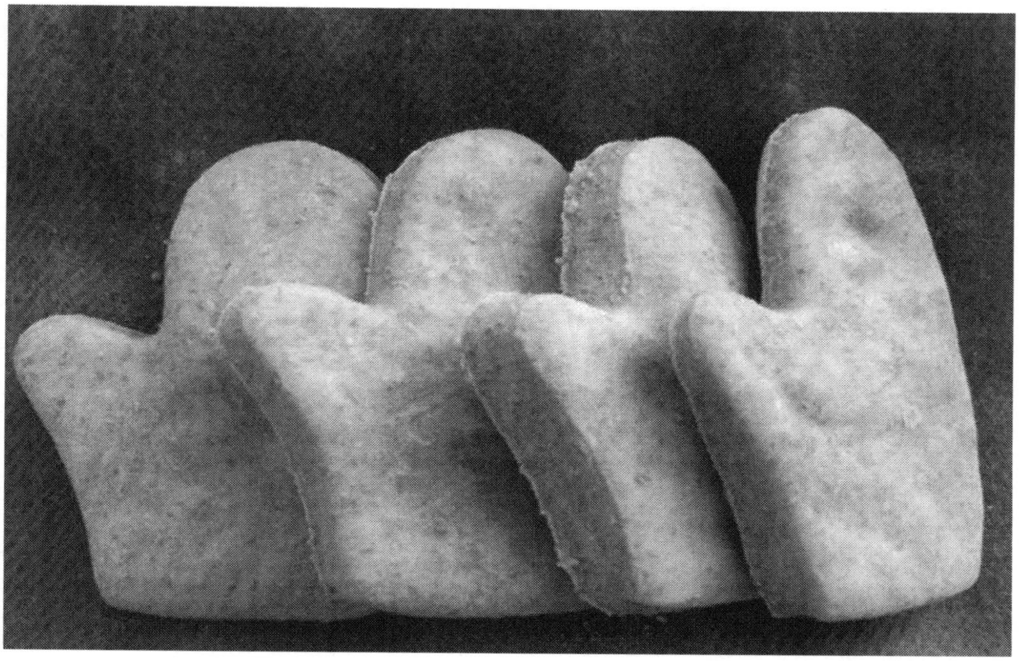

Instructions:

Preheat oven to 350 degrees.

In a large bowl, mix flour, molasses, peanut butter, water, olive oil and peppermint extract until smooth.

Kneed flour on a floured surface and roll out to ¼ inch thickness. Cut with festive cookie cutters and place on non-stick cookie sheets.

Bake for 30 minutes. Cool on wire rack. Store treats in a sealed container and refrigerate or freeze.

Tuesday

December 15th, 2020

6 am	
7	
8	
9	
10	
11	
12 pm	
1	
2	
3	
4	
5	
6	
7	
8	

PRIORITIES

TO DO

NOTES:

Wednesday

December 16th, 2020

6 am	
7	
8	
9	
10	
11	
12 pm	
1	
2	
3	
4	
5	
6	
7	
8	

PRIORITIES

TO DO

NOTES:

Thursday

December 17th, 2020

6 am	
7	
8	
9	
10	
11	
12 pm	
1	
2	
3	
4	
5	
6	
7	
8	

PRIORITIES

TO DO

NOTES:

Friday

December 18th, 2020

6 am	
7	
8	
9	
10	
11	
12 pm	
1	
2	
3	
4	
5	
6	
7	
8	

PRIORITIES

TO DO

NOTES:

Saturday

December 19th, 2020

6 am	
7	
8	
9	
10	
11	
12 pm	
1	
2	
3	
4	
5	
6	
7	
8	

PRIORITIES

TO DO

NOTES:

Sunday

December 20th, 2020

6 am	
7	
8	
9	
10	
11	
12 pm	
1	
2	
3	
4	
5	
6	
7	
8	

PRIORITIES

TO DO

NOTES:

Monday

December 21st, 2020

6 am	
7	
8	
9	
10	
11	
12 pm	
1	
2	
3	
4	
5	
6	
7	
8	

PRIORITIES

TO DO

NOTES:

Tuesday

December 22nd, 2020

6 am	
7	
8	
9	
10	
11	
12 pm	
1	
2	
3	
4	
5	
6	
7	
8	

PRIORITIES

TO DO

NOTES:

Wednesday

December 23rd, 2020

6 am	
7	
8	
9	
10	
11	
12 pm	
1	
2	
3	
4	
5	
6	
7	
8	

PRIORITIES

TO DO

NOTES:

Thursday

December 24th, 2020

6 am	
7	
8	
9	
10	
11	
12 pm	
1	
2	
3	
4	
5	
6	
7	
8	

PRIORITIES

TO DO

NOTES:

Friday

December 25th, 2020

6 am	
7	
8	
9	
10	
11	
12 pm	
1	
2	
3	
4	
5	
6	
7	
8	

PRIORITIES

TO DO

NOTES:

Saturday

December 26th, 2020

6 am	
7	
8	
9	
10	
11	
12 pm	
1	
2	
3	
4	
5	
6	
7	
8	

PRIORITIES

TO DO

NOTES:

Sunday

December 27th, 2020

6 am	
7	
8	
9	
10	
11	
12 pm	
1	
2	
3	
4	
5	
6	
7	
8	

PRIORITIES

TO DO

NOTES:

Monday

December 28th, 2020

6 am	
7	
8	
9	
10	
11	
12 pm	
1	
2	
3	
4	
5	
6	
7	
8	

PRIORITIES

TO DO

NOTES:

Tuesday

December 29th, 2020

6 am	
7	
8	
9	
10	
11	
12 pm	
1	
2	
3	
4	
5	
6	
7	
8	

PRIORITIES

TO DO

NOTES:

Wednesday

December 30th, 2020

6 am	
7	
8	
9	
10	
11	
12 pm	
1	
2	
3	
4	
5	
6	
7	
8	

PRIORITIES

TO DO

NOTES:

Thursday

December 31st, 2020

6 am	
7	
8	
9	
10	
11	
12 pm	
1	
2	
3	
4	
5	
6	
7	
8	

PRIORITIES

TO DO

NOTES:

Notes...

I just had the best walk ever!

I saw 35 or 4 other dogs...

woofers, thick bois, a loaf, even a floofer pupper.

Life is good!

THE TIRED HAS COME.
BIG SNOOZE AWAITS
BEFORE I GO.
PLEASE NOTE...
I LOVE YOU SO MUCH,
HOOMAN.

Made in the USA
Middletown, DE
14 October 2020

21900182R00247